PRAISE FOR *PYRE*

'Murugan's fictional villages are places full of quiet menace, where caste boundaries are protected with violence and social exclusion . . . [*Pyre* is] so tense it leaves you gasping for air' —Ellen Barry, *New York Times*

'*Pyre* glows with as much power as [*One Part Woman*] did, and adds immeasurable value to contemporary Indian literature . . . "Meditative, joyous, humbling"—three words [that] describe perfectly the sensations with which you put down Perumal Murugan's *Pyre*, a book marked with the same quality of luminous integrity and beauty seen in *One Part Woman* . . . Aniruddhan translates with a fine ear that preserves beautifully the music of the original . . . [Murugan] succeeds in universalising Kongu Nadu to such a degree that place and person fall away and all that remains is a hard and glittering gem of a story'—Vaishna Roy, *The Hindu*

'[A] sensitive, richly textured translation by Aniruddhan Vasudevan . . . Murugan writes with a gentle, sensual tenderness that is unforgettable [and also] with cinematic power, and the final images of *Pyre* will sear your heart, though he makes sure that the reader writes the ending with him . . . *One Part Woman* was met with intolerance of such a degree that it forced him into silence. *Pyre*, written before the storm of bigotry swept through the author's life, is even more accomplished, bitterly haunting, a love story, and an indictment of those who hate with such staunch righteousness'—Nilanjana Roy, *Business Standard*

'The prose is deceptively simple and sparse. And yet it has the effect of hitting you hard like the blazing sun . . . [Murugan]

knows how to handle masterful imagery and human emotions. Especially when he delves into the emotional space of his women characters, be it a coarse, unloving mother-in-law or the soft, sparrow-like, bewildered new bride . . . A sensitive translation done with great care. There is not a single word that jars . . . [Pyre] will haunt the reader for a long time'
—Vaasanthi, *Indian Express*

'The real fire in *Pyre* [lies] in Murugan's words . . . Aniruddhan Vasudevan [translates] the story of *Pyre* beautifully . . . With *Pyre*, Murugan places a love story at the centre of human confusion and regional literature at the centre of Indian mainstream writing'—*Financial Express*

'A poignant love story . . . Murugan vividly describes the dusty, beautiful landscape and through his characters gives us a peek into the daily struggles and joys of a different kind of life'—*Femina*

PRAISE FOR *ONE PART WOMAN*

'A superb book in which tenderness, love and desire kindle each other into a conflagration of sexual rapture'—Bapsi Sidhwa

'Perumal Murugan opens up the layers of desire, longing, loss and fulfilment in a relationship with extraordinary sensitivity and surgical precision'—Ambai

'A fable about sexual passion and social norms, pleasure and the conventions of family and motherhood . . . A lovely rendering of the Tamil'—*Biblio*

'Perumal Murugan turns an intimate and crystalline gaze on a married couple in interior Tamil Nadu. It is a gaze that lays bare the intricacies of their story, culminating in a heart-wrenching denouement that allows no room for apathy . . . *One Part Woman* is a powerful and insightful rendering of an entire milieu which is certainly still in existence. [Murugan] handles myriad complexities with an enviable sophistication, creating an evocative, even haunting, work . . . Murugan's writing is taut and suspenseful . . . Aniruddhan Vasudevan's translation deserves mention—the language is crisp, retaining local flavour without jarring, and often lyrical'—*The Hindu Business Line*

'An evocative novel about a childless couple reminds us of the excellence of writing in Indian languages . . . This is a novel of many layers; of richly textured relationships; of raw and resonant dialogues and characters . . . Perumal Murugan's voice is distinct; it is the voice of writing in the Indian languages rich in characters, dialogues and locales that are unerringly drawn and intensely evocative. As the novel moves towards its inevitable climax, tragic yet redemptive, the reader shares in the anguish of the characters caught in a fate beyond their control. It is because a superb writer has drawn us adroitly into the lives of those far removed from our acquaintance'—*Indian Express*

'Murugan imbues the simple story of a young couple, deeply in love and anxious to have a child, with the complexities of convention, obligation and, ultimately, conviction . . . An engaging story'—*Time Out*

'*One Part Woman* has the distant romanticism of a gentler, slower, prettier world, but it is infused with a sense of immediacy . . . Murugan intricately examines the effect the pressure to have a child has on [the couple's] relationship . . . *One Part Woman* is beautifully rooted in its setting. Murugan delights in description and Aniruddhan translates it ably' —*Open*

PRAISE FOR PERUMAL MURUGAN

'Versatile, sensitive to history and conscious of his responsibilities as a writer, Murugan is . . . the most accomplished of his generation of Tamil writers'—*Caravan*

'[A] great literary chronicler . . . Murugan is at the height of his creative powers'—*The Hindu*

'Murugan's insights about relationships spread throughout his work like flashes of lightning'—*Kalachuvadu*

'The Tamil Irvine Welsh'—*Guardian*

PENGUIN BOOKS

SONGS OF A COWARD

Perumal Murugan is the star of contemporary Tamil literature. An award-winning writer, poet and scholar, he has garnered both critical acclaim and commercial success for his vast array of work. Some of his novels have been translated into English to immense acclaim, including *Seasons of the Palm*, which was shortlisted for the Kiriyama Prize in 2005, and *One Part Woman*, his best-known work, which was shortlisted for the Crossword Award and won the prestigious ILF Samanvay Bhasha Samman in 2015.

Aniruddhan Vasudevan is a performer, writer, translator and PhD student in anthropology at the University of Texas, Austin. His much-lauded translation of Perumal Murugan's *One Part Woman* won the Sahitya Akademi Award in 2016 and the Tamil Literary Garden's (Canada) Best Translation Award in 2013.

SONGS OF A COWARD

poems of exile

PERUMAL MURUGAN

TRANSLATED BY ANIRUDDHAN VASUDEVAN

PENGUIN BOOKS

An imprint of Penguin Random House

PENGUIN BOOKS

USA | Canada | UK | Ireland | Australia
New Zealand | India | South Africa | China | Singapore

Penguin Books is part of the Penguin Random House group of companies
whose addresses can be found at global.penguinrandomhouse.com

Published by Penguin Random House India Pvt. Ltd
4th Floor, Capital Tower 1, MG Road,
Gurugram 122 002, Haryana, India

First published in Tamil as *Kozhaiyin Paadalgal* by Kalachuvadu
Publications Pvt. Ltd, Nagercoil 2016
First published in English in Penguin Books by Penguin Random House India 2017

Copyright © Perumal Murugan 2016, 2017
English translation copyright © Aniruddhan Vasudevan 2017

10 9 8 7 6 5 4 3 2

ISBN 9780143428824

Typeset in Adobe Caslon Pro by Manipal Digital Systems, Manipal

Printed at Manipal Technologies Limited, India

www.penguin.co.in

MIX
Paper | Supporting
responsible forestry
FSC® C043100

This is a legitimate digitally printed version of the book and therefore might not
have certain extra finishing on the cover.

Contents

Introduction

It Seeped in All Directions

I am familiar with dryland agriculture. I know how to take cattle to graze. I also have some experience running a soda-drink shop. And I have done some magazine publishing work as well. For twenty years now, I have been a full-time teacher.

However, writing is my true vocation. Even when I was really young, I discovered that writing was my calling. It has kept me company, and allowed me to share things with myself. It has also helped me keep myself at a distance, gain some perspective. Writing has even given me the pleasure of moving forward and back in time. It has allowed me to become a spring bird and merge my voice with that of the present.

Never have I not been engaged in the act of writing.

Of course, the pressures of material life have kept me from writing now and then. But even then my mind was always ticking with ideas. I don't know whether I had the ability to stem the flow of my thoughts and exert control over them. But I know I never felt any desire to rein them in. Many of those thoughts just ran away and never came back. There have also been those that only appeared to run away but actually stayed buried inside and later expressed themselves when I put pen to paper. Writing to me is a habit of the mind. And poetry is my ideal. It is close to my inner being. Right or wrong, it allows me to give vent to my feelings and emotions.

Poetry, to me, is a vehicle to recover from anything. No matter how stressful the situation, I have been able to endure it, hanging on to the tip of the one word that takes shape in my mind. This habit of talking to myself sometimes even manifests in the movement of my lips, when my thoughts are given shape as spoken words. That has caused some amount of trouble in the outside world. And there are many lone words and phrases that have never got written down. While it is true that I cannot take pride in every such word that takes shape in my mind, I had always thought of this mental habit as a boon.

But there came a moment when I realized this boon was a curse, and I stifled it. I thought I was done with it, that I could perform the final rites for it and get on with my life. But I couldn't. I felt like a dead man walking, though there was nothing I could do about it. I had throttled the voice, killed it. I hoped that I'd soon stop grieving. But that did not happen either. Perhaps I was not strong enough to kill. Thus, for a long while my mental habit lay ailing. But finally it rose with a roar and possessed me again—words, thoughts, poetry. And then it seeped in all directions like an unstoppable spring.

When I found an opportunity, I set the words down on paper. They kept coming forth like never before. Poetry is a great medicine, a rare herb. It was poetry that revived me.

* * *

A great friend I made during the year and a half I spent in Chennai is Srinivasan Natarajan, who is an artist, a painter. During this period, he wrote the novel *Vidambanam* for me. It was the poet Atmanam's death anniversary the day after I wrote the poem 'Judgement Day', which is included in this collection (6 July 2016). On that day, a group of us friends gathered on Marina Beach. That was when Srinivasan requested me to write another poem, a new one after

'Judgement Day', which I did. That poem now finds a place in his novel. It was also he who designed the cover for the Tamil edition of this book.

I had taught my father, who was not literate, how to sign his name. I don't have even a single photo of him—only a signature of his on my class ten register. Looking at it has always given me the feeling that I am looking at him. Srinivasan wonderfully recreated that signature and used it on the cover of the Tamil edition. I am thankful to his creativity.

The poet Sukumaran read and responded to these poems. He is a touchstone for me—one that enhances without distorting. My affectionate thanks to him and to Kannan at Kalachuvadu who was very keen on publishing this book.

In a way, this is a first book for me. So there is a long list of people I should thank. This book is an expression of a feeling that is beyond gratitude in its depth. I dedicate this book to everyone who stood by me in difficult times.

Perumal Murugan

Translator's Note

The circumstances under which Perumal Murugan wrote the Tamil poems whose English translations you find in this book are well known now. Following the controversy and psychic violence stirred up around his novel *Madhorubhagan* (which I had translated into English as *One Part Woman*), Perumal Murugan announced his own death as an author and withdrew from public life for a while. I saw that moment as the withdrawal of a writer's love and trust from a world that was tormenting him.

He wrote these poems during that period of exile when he was struggling to find his bearings, trying to make sense of all that was happening in his life and how it might affect his existence as a person and writer. We clearly hear the journaling voice in these poems; they record private emotions, acute vulnerability and a constant sense of cautiously moving around a space to see how hospitable, inhabitable and welcoming it might be—or not.

I like some of the poems more than I like the others. But I think that's because I found a greater ease with translating some than I did with others. I have tried my best to retain the simplicity of his poetic syntax, the starkness of his phrasing and imagery and the directness of his voice. I have also kept in mind that these poems document a turbulent period in the life of a writer who has experienced serious curtailment of his artistic freedom at the hands of caste and religious bigotry. So they record for us the inner life of a writer who is hurt, who is thankful for the wonderful support he has received but who has taken a step back to see how he would function in the world henceforth—as a writer and poet, as a person with a strong sense of belonging to a place, as a husband and father, as a teacher, as a friend, as a social being who exists in the criss-crossing of these and various other relationships and encounters.

For Perumal Murugan, these encounters happen not only with other humans. He has an acute awareness of the space around him and the various things that animate that space. Beetles, spiders, plants, dogs, pigs, rats, pigeons, trees, snails, windows, doors, goats, sheep, light, shadow, heat, humidity, dryness, voices, silences—all these are pulled into the orbit of his thoughts and musings, not as mere props but as entities that go into the making of moments, connections and relationships.

These poems, private reflections though they are, mark an important moment in our collective self-reflection about the nature of a literary public we might wish to create for ourselves and how vigilant we should stay against the forces of censorship and the curtailment of freedom of thought and expression.

July 2017   Aniruddhan Vasudevan
Chennai

SONGS
OF A
COWARD

1 Thousands and Thousands

I enter the body
of a guinea pig poisoned to death
As if waking suddenly
from a dream
it looks terrified
at the vastness around

It runs amok in panic
and burrows a hole
under a wide bank

As it digs out sand from the hole
wind and light fall on its skin
It shudders, shrinks
and burrows in quickly

Thousands and thousands of pathways
Thousands and thousands of dead ends

Holed up somewhere
no one can find
Where am I right now?

22 FEBRUARY 2015

2 A Great Stream

Nameless, endless
impassable forest

Alone, a lamb bounds about
making new pathways
as it runs

As it runs
it leaps
to cross a great stream
that has appeared suddenly

It is possible
that it would cross the stream
and look back in wonder
It is possible
that it would falter in its leap
and fall in and die

May the wide-mouthed stream
do right
by the lamb

22 FEBRUARY 2015

3 A Glimpse

In my land of endless drought
a miracle occurs

When I hear the howl, I think
it is the wind's rage
An army of white snakes
comes frothing like a wave
and sweeps me away

As I stand balancing
on the wave's crest
I catch a glimpse of the sky

Then
the wave curls
and tucks me within itself

22 FEBRUARY 2015

4   A Strange Beast

My very existence becomes a threat
to anyone I meet

As soon as I enter
they close doors and windows
As soon as they see me
they hurriedly send away their guests
They drift away from my words
and look anxiously around
They fall silent
They make plans to send me away quickly

They text from their cell phones under the table
informing God knows who about my visit
They take photos with me
and leave
They try to make a rare wonder
of my voice

Someone has painted over my head
a pair of horns everyone can see
Someone has turned me
into a strange beast

22 FEBRUARY 2015

5 A Drop of Bother

for Shahjahan

I inconvenience everyone

The one who bore the brunt of it
simply because I was unruly
was my mother

It brings suffering
to my wife and children too

Those inconvenienced
by a single sentence from my pen
gift me shoe-showers

For some, my beard is an inconvenience
For some, my clothes are an inconvenience
For some, my acts are an inconvenience
For some, my growth is an inconvenience
For some, my speech is an inconvenience
For some, my writing is an inconvenience
For some, my existence is an inconvenience

I only wish to vanish
and stop
being an inconvenience to anyone

But
a drop of my inconvenience

might have fallen on you too
You bore it patiently
Thank you for your true love

23 FEBRUARY 2015

6 News of a Cremation

That day, the road turned into a cremation ground

Those who came to light the pyre
with claims to inheritance
had flames for fingers
Writings burnt and blended into the air

First, all activities ceased
Then, one day, final rites too were done

Now
I wish to remind you
of your own words

Body dies
Soul doesn't

23 FEBRUARY 2015

7   Names of Days

Names of days
have become ruins of antiquity
We can give them new names
by flinging up new words
from the warehouse of language

Week, month, year
all such calculations too will go obsolete
Even day

Instead
We shall name a day Cuckoo's Call
We shall name a day Scattering of Snow
We shall name a day Stone's Softening
We shall name a day Mountain Peak
We shall name a day Crescent Moon

Each unlike the other, each unlike the other
So many days

We shall name some days
Devil's Scream
Fool's Grunt
Corpse's Stench
And get past them easily

23 FEBRUARY 2015

8   A Language without Nouns

All that get caught like cobwebs in the broom
of the man who set out to cleanse language
are nouns

He keeps clearing away
at the reeking mass
that are the names of people
Trash piles up high

Names of places go into the pile
along with names of people

Nouns for things, nouns for time
Nouns for qualities, nouns for body parts
Nothing survives

Now
only verbs leap about
all over the dictionary

Conceding to the pleadings
of the language-mother who stands frozen
he magnanimously allows some nouns
but not the ones for people
and the places they live in

Unable to bear the sting
of her entreaties

he allows pronouns too
and sets the broom down
in a corner.

23 FEBRUARY 2015

9 With a Poem

Even as he falls shattered
like twigs from a nest undone
he feels
that everything could be set right
with a poem

Plenty of poems
lie in front of him
He gathers up
as much as he can

He intercepts an officer
and recites him a poem
Stunned at first
the man then runs, turning to look back
over and over
He thinks the officer
must have understood the poem

He recites poetry
to his family, relatives
and friends
He recites poetry
to strangers, men, women
children, the young and the old
to everyone

At the entrance to the town, at the temple gates
at the foot of the hill, at the bus stand

on the streets, on the roadsides
he recites poetry

Those who observe him for a while
smile, thinking he is insane
Some are shocked

Some others listen to his poems keenly
and with the freshness of a new dawn
his hope grows stronger

23 FEBRUARY 2015

10 Touch-Me-Not

A seed set down by time
on that dry land
came to life one rainy day
sprouted a Touch-me-not
that blossomed with surprising lushness

No one knew of its greatness
When a pale red blossom appeared
an innocent boy looked at in wonder
When he reached to pluck the flower
the leaves shuddered and closed
He quickly touched all the leaves
The plant drew the leaves in
as if it were dead

He brought his friends
to show them this wonder
The leaves had opened up by then

He touched them gently with a finger
The leaves shuddered and shrank
Another touched with his foot
The leaves shuddered and shrank

One boy touched them with his shoes
The leaves shuddered and shrank
Another touched them with a stick
The leaves shuddered and shrank

Yet another touched with his lips
The leaves shuddered and shrank
and closed themselves completely

They waited
When the first leaf unfolded
one of them touched it
with his threatening voice
It shuddered and shrank

After that, the touch of their voices was enough
Not a single leaf unfurled

23 FEBRUARY 2015

11 Surrender

I
bring a flower
You
bring a sword

Not only a fight
Even peace is not possible
Only surrender
Total surrender

Go ahead and declare your victory
Clap your hands and whistle
Dance, celebrate, rejoice

Your
kindness and pity
are not towards the one ostracized

I am standing a little aside
just watching
the flower that is getting crushed
under your feet
that don't touch the ground

1 FEBRUARY 2015

12 A Rented House

Mostly
we live only in rented houses
That's what is convenient too

It is easy to swiftly inhabit something
that someone built at some point
for someone else

If it smells of the old
some new paint will do
All we need to do
is to go into the ready rooms
and look for nails on which to hang things
on the walls, in the corners, in the almirahs

We can easily sweep away
the footprints and the layers of dust

We can quickly get past
without a moment's hesitation
even the occasional feeling
that we are only living
in a rented house

After all, isn't the whole world a rented place?

12 MARCH 2015

13 Own House

How can we enjoy the house we own?

We can drive nails wherever we want
We can accumulate things
give them permanent places
without the nagging feeling
that we will have to move one day

We can show our guests around with pride
with quick comebacks to their comments
about its Vaastu shortcomings
We can ponder how our house is different
from others
Front room, bedroom, kitchen
and if there is a little more space
a dining hall and a prayer room
But
the colour we have painted is different
That choice is entirely ours

14 MARCH 2015

17

14 A New House

A house never stays new
We make it so by saying over and over
that it is new

We change the curtains regularly
We use new chemicals
to remove finger stains from the walls

We spend all our holidays
caring for the house

We delight in the things our guests say—
It is as good as new
It looks just like a new house
Is it new? It is!

We use the same tricks on the house
that an ageing man does on himself—
Combing his hair forward
to cover his baldness
Colouring his hair
to hide the greying

A house never stays new

15 MARCH 2015

15 Definitely a Rat

It was they who discovered
that I was a rat

I did not know I was one
So I sat, clueless, watching
their preparations
to catch a rat

They sent out fliers, printed posters
with my photo, calling me a rat
But I bore no resemblance
to a rat

When they grasped my neck with tongs
and lifted me up
I felt the movement of my tail
and realized I was indeed a rat

Now I lie on a table
legs spread out
and nailed down
I am definitely a rat
A lab rat

14 MARCH 2015

16 A Baby Crow

No matter where I go
I am bad at directions
In this big city, every step
is confusing

'Befriend someone,' says an astral voice
Electric trains, buses, cars, motorbikes
Everyone going about their ways
Any friendly smile lasts
only as long as the traffic lights do

After wandering around looking
for a face to befriend
on a hot afternoon of rejections
I noticed the crows

I chose a black-necked, swollen-headed crow
that came and sat on top of the old door
in my office and cawed away
We found the rhythm of friendship in just four to five
     days

I held its fanned tail and crossed streets
got into buses, went everywhere
from supermarkets to petty shops
I raked garbage
I walked avoiding the river of sewage

When I grew thirsty

the crow took me to the top
of a tall building where
a water tank sat cross-legged
The crow sat on a pipe that drained
excess water from the tank
It bent gracefully, sucked in some water
in its beak and fed it to me
I opened my mouth and received it eagerly
like a baby crow

22 MARCH 2015

17 A Divine Tongue

I am angry enough
to sing a song of curses
at all of you

I am angry enough to curse
that the hands that burnt my effigy
shall char in the same fire
That the words that flew at me
like poison-soaked arrows
shall turn back to go
and wound and kill
the stone hearts that sent them

I am angry enough to sing
Oh you guardians of morals
May the screens part
and expose your truths
May the lord of cremation grounds
dance, smearing the ashes
from your powdered bones

I am angry enough to sing
a song of curses
That lips that spout lies shall burn and wither
That crowds that gather quickly shall die

But my divine tongue has no words
for curses
Go away, live!

26 MARCH 2015

18 An Exhibit

I stand as a live exhibit
Hands grope about my head
looking to see if I have horns
When I lower my head obligingly
they move away in fear

I stand inside a glass cage
out of anyone's reach
But their gazes keep moving over me
looking for differences

I expose my canines
and stick out my tongue
They shudder and run

Most of my time passes
in trying to attract the attention
of feet that go by uninterested
thinking I am just another display

At night, nothing but loneliness

It is not easy
getting used to being
an exhibition piece

26 MARCH 2015

19 Those with Hands

When they come with closed hands
there is a sharp knife hidden there

When they come with open hands
it is a trick to conceal weapons
in their clothes or in their mouths

When they come with folded hands
there is definitely a dagger concealed there

If a bag of fruits or snacks
hangs from their hands
they are sure to be poisoned

When they extend their hands to shake mine
I decline, calling it a foreign custom
Fingers are saw-teeth
Anything can happen when
they pull and embrace me

Forgive me
But anyone with hands
is suspect

28 MARCH 2015

20 The Headless Ones

There are headless people all over town
The sculptor kneads and kneads his clay
and makes innumerable heads
for them to try on

Like children who cast off their clothes
and roam around
people cast away the heads

Heads lie scattered in the streets
Unfazed, the sculptor makes
new heads with exquisite faces

Hoping to entice women
some young men eagerly wear them
But in an instant
the faces flatten, fall apart

No heads fit those headless bodies
that come thinking
that a head might mean a chance to bear the crown

Wearied, the sculptor gives up
Headless people roam around town
gleefully

29 MARCH 2015

21 Fortunate

It has been years since my mother died
Every day, for at least a minute
I wish
she had lived a little longer

I'd have had
someone to bear without a murmur
a sliver of my burdens
I'd have had
someone to rightfully chasten
fight with, get angry at

A vein of love would have run
deep like the mark etched
by a piece of thread on wet concrete

It is just as well she is gone
She is fortunate
not to see her child
struggle like a little bird
tossed about, wings torn
caught in a storm

15 APRIL 2015

22 Snail Shells

They say the snail carries on its back
sins of several former lives
A good armour
for such a pitiable creature
with a soft body and hollow horns

Even the touch of leaves and twigs
sends it huddling inside

Cast away your burden of sins—
they command it
It's just a cage of calcium—
they tease

The snail too
tries to shed its shell
But poor creature
Its congenital baggage
has sucked up blood
and hardened

Time pokes at it with a needle
pulls out its body and
tosses it on a sun-scorched tar road

Everywhere the stench of its singe
Vehicle tyres have ground
and smeared it away
without a trace

Now you can see snails
only behind glass cases
From now on snail shells
will stay absolutely still

14 APRIL 2015

23 Force of Habit

Enemies who lay in wait
setting thorns on my path
ambushed me
one harsh afternoon

Startled at first
I soon found my bearings

By force of habit
my hand moved to my waist

On my stylish belt
hung
a shadow-sword

1 APRIL 2015

24 Cowardice

The king decided
to have all cowards killed

Everyone became a warrior
Roars resounded everywhere
Human bodies stood erect
like the earth's genitals

As unsheathed swords swayed in the wind
cowardice lay
enjoying its siesta
in the scabbard

When the sheath was opened
to slide the swords back in
it leapt out like a mouse
and roamed about
in the dark

1 APRIL 2015

25 I Did Not Know It Was the Devil

This is the devil that possessed me
at birth
Until now
it hadn't revealed itself as the devil

It was not interested in playing
It wouldn't let me close to anyone
Sweeping me in its wide merciful arms
it would drop me in the wild
and caress me with its beautiful hands

Sometimes I'd sprout butterfly wings
Sometimes I'd grow a honeybird's bent beak
Sometimes I'd stand on crane legs
Tiger's leap at times
Deer's fright at times
Sometimes, a kite's vision
Sometimes, a cuckoo's red eyes

Before I'd grow weary
it'd make me light as a feather
and bring me back
When it chose to turn into a stifling ghost
it'd press me into a deep slumber
where I knew no hunger nor thirst

Laziness was its invaluable gift
When I'd hurl insults
and strangle its throat in mock anger

it'd laugh and twirl and leap
on to a tamarind tree branch
and shake words free from there
My treasure trove would overflow

Until now, I didn't know it was the devil

A priest has come from somewhere
He whirls his whip
binds me with enchanted ropes
casts spells to chase it out
grows a fire to burn it in
I pity my devil
The devil that is me

5 APRIL 2015

26 Electric Fire

Shivering in the Margazhi chill
I held my hands open in front of the cinder
that sparked invitingly late at night
At once, it grasped and burnt my hand
Funeral fire
Formless mouths broke and ate
pieces of my hands
that burnt along with the firewood

I pressed my feet
on cow-dung patties
stacked up in the summer
My feet cooked to perfection
in the fragrant fire
Mysterious beaks pecked and swallowed it

I gave my body to burn
in the stench of blazing tyres
its black smoke swirling skyward
The fingers of waiting hordes
tore at me hot and fresh
like I was a palmyra fruit

That's how it has been so far
Now
I will descend into the electric fire
that no hands can reach

I will fuse with the air
leaving not even ashes

6 APRIL 2015

27 Filter

In my childhood, I was called *pannadai**
palm-sheath filter
I filtered toddy and sap
I drank my fill when they lingered in me
before they trickled down
Thinking of the meaningful life
of bees, beetles and ants
that stayed caught in them
I sighed
and was left with an emptiness

In my youth, I became
finely made perfect little filters
I took various shapes
different colours
Each day
a different look
I was entranced
by my own appearance
I filtered toddy and tea
and ghee
but nothing lingered
and dropped down slowly
It was all quick
Once I tasted even a little

---

* *Pannadai* refers to the filter made from a palm sheath.
Colloquially, it also means a fool.

on the tip of my tongue
I was impatient for the next thing

Now, middle-aged, I still stand
as a large, gaping filter
whose rim I can't even see
Only water falls and escapes
Here I stand
as a gigantic filter
that adamantly clings on to sorrows
and lets happiness trickle away

7 APRIL 2015

28 Enough Is Enough

You fill my plate with food
You make it tastier, more fragrant
You roll out the royal carpet for me
You shower me with rose petals
You give me nectar to drink
You wipe my lips with a soft towel
You shower me with praise
You put me on a pedestal

Enough is enough

Stop all of this
Including
your antics behind my back

8 APRIL 2015

29 The Only Sound

Until now, I have struggled
not knowing this little trick
Until now, I have been ears
only for the songs of birds
turned only towards music

Like festival loudspeakers
that can be turned any which way
I have now turned my ears
towards human speech

In the clamour of words
my ears have grown bigger
and my lips have fallen silent
like the leaves of a great tree

Now the only word
No
The only sound
my lips know
is
mm

8 APRIL 2015

30 The Song of a Coward

Misery befalls no one
because of a coward
Riots break out nowhere
because of a coward
Nothing is ever ruined
because of a coward

A coward
never draws his sword
never aims it at a tree to test its sharpness
In fact, a coward never carries a sword

No one is threatened
by a coward

A coward
is scared of darkness
Songs come forth from him

A coward
is fearful of daylight
Poetry comes forth from him

Nature welcomes a coward
He doesn't nip a leaf
or pluck a flower

Nature embraces a coward
A mother always suckles

her shivering child

Nature celebrates a coward
He steps out only to feed himself
He upsets nothing since he keeps to himself

A coward also finds it hard
to stay cooped up in the house
He keeps busy
repairing nooks and corners

You won't find a coward in the playground
He never allows himself to be swept up
in nationalistic fervour

A coward
never joins political parties
follows no ideology
is loyal to no leader

A coward
can't make posters
can't bathe cut-outs with milk
He simply cannot
whistle and prance
and join processions

A coward does not steal from anyone
He causes no trouble to those
who steal from him

A coward
does not attempt rape
He is unable to glance secretly
at anyone's body

A coward
never turns into a murderer
But
he does think about suicide
and does it, too

12 APRIL 2015

31 Right Here

This world refuses to grant
pasture to a goat
sky to a bird
water to a fish

We are forced to live
right here
in this world

10 AUGUST 2015

32 An Endless Trove

Vacating a house is not easy

Since an empty house lacks dignity
we keep buying things
to fill it up

Though we grow tired of it at times
whenever we see a new thing
we consider seriously
where it might belong in the house

We even find space
for old things
A house's strength are its things

A house is an endless trove of things

As we keep emptying
things just keep coming out
We never manage to empty a house

8 APRIL 2015

33 Footprints

Dust completely shrouds
everything in my house

I have arrived too late
I walk over the dust
I leave footprints
I run all over the house
Footprints, footprints

Once I realize
that the house has preserved
my footprints
even under the dust I have not set foot on
I calm down

11 JUNE 2015

34 The Spade

God bequeathed to me
love
in the form of a spade

Like a farmer at the fair
appraising his purchase
I examined carefully
the heavy metal rim
and the reddened wood handle

I was always attracted
to a spade's wide rim
that sparkled like sun on water

I was delighted
I could use the spade
over the earth's wide expanses

I trimmed and made neat bunds
I consoled the grasses for their singed roots
and fed them to the cows
I made sure there was water for the trees
I dug water channels
I set right the slopes

I asked the spade
to take from the swell
and give to the pit
In this, I spent most of my time

One sleepless night
when I looked for it
under my bed where I'd kept it safe
edges scraped and washed
I couldn't find the spade

I hear a noise outside
It is digging a pit
for me

15 APRIL 2015

35 Encroachment

From under the tree
I picked up
a cannonball flower

Loosened phallus
but erect serpent hoods
bent, falling
like an umbrella
Pungent, seminal odour

I placed the flower on my table
admired it
and dozed off

The odour pervaded
The umbrella unfurled inside the room
When I wake up
I am lying breathless
under its canopy

36 A Poor Little Beetle

How did this little beetle get in?
Through the gap in the roof
the hole in the window net
the chink in the door
or with someone when they entered
It has somehow entered this space
this beetle

Its hum
bores into my head

It struggles to find the way it came in
There are several possibilities
but it is unable to find one

It bangs against the ridge of the ceiling
It halts where it finds light
but turns back

Its humming escalates
I am scared it might sting me
in its frenzied flying

I rush
and open the door and windows
But the beetle can't find its way out

I step outside
When I go back in

after giving it some time
it is still swirling around
That little beetle

Who has sent it?
What if it stakes a claim here?

I am going to be patient no longer
With my weapons—
a long towel
a hand fan and
a blanket—
I get ready for war

It can't be spared,
can it?
The poor little beetle

37 The Dance of Creation

What do I do with this?

It's not a person but a venomous snake
Snakes carry venom in their teeth

It's not a snake but pure venom
Venom's power is to destroy

It's not venom but the dance of creation

I roll it up and
stuff it inside
layers and layers of baskets
But it stands up defiantly
pushing open
even the strongest of baskets

What it needs
is a vastness to twirl around in

But what can I do?
I can only offer a basket
woven tightly with wire

38 Snails

Snails
are my only amusement

I feel excited
when they crawl out
on quiet days

I poke them
with whatever I can find
a stick, a wire, a needle
Touch-me-nots
They even have horns
with little mushroom tops
Pointless protrusions
I can nudge with my fingers

I can pick them up easily
And hurl them on little rocks
They have protective shells
little calcium boxes

On days I can't find snails
I simply look
in the mirror

39 Word Game

In the loft in my house
I found an old *pallaankuzhi* game-board
and some words I had flung there
for later use

Playfully
I separated the words into groups
and dropped them
in the cups on the game-board

The cup of pleading words
spills over
The cup of helplessness too
has several expletives floating in it

Words of agreement aren't too many
but they too keep falling into their cup

I look carefully for words of peace
and take them to their cup
They only fill a little over half

Words of affection are mostly rusty
Only a few broken and faulty ones remain

One empty cup remains
that I can lick and claim
That is where I plan to drop
my words of resistance

40 A Full-Body Shave

The king has decreed
that humans shall be skinned alive

They dig out
old blunt, broken shaving knives

Those who have managed to obtain knives
are running around
screaming

Blunt knives
that can't even make a scratch
on thick leather
are now looking for soft skin

Children
and artists
are the soft-skinned ones

Children
should be skinned in secret
says the order

Children are gathered together
and made to watch
artists being skinned
right in front of them

A knife scrapes the skin off their faces
Another targets the palms of their hands
Yet another slices into their backs

Then they drop sun-dried pieces of skin
in the children's hands
who tremble and weep
and shut their eyes and shrink within

And the artists stand
dripping blood
from searing wounds
and pretending that
they are just getting
a full-body shave

4 JUNE 2015

41 The Spider's Target

The spider has woven its web
like a banner
stretching from a tree on one side
to a tree on the other side
of a wide path

No one knows
which corner, which weave
how big, how small
In fact
the spider is not there at all
It does not live in its web

But its eyes
keep watch from somewhere

Many who cross the road
in broad daylight
don't seem to notice the web
If they looked carefully in the evening
they might see it in the stir of its threads
But who has the time

Small bugs, little insects
beetles, butterflies
dragonflies—
there are many that get caught
struggle and die in the web

From somewhere
the spider's eyes
observe everything

The spider
is not going to emerge for now
Its target
is bigger
very big
bigger than the biggest
A human hand

7 JUNE 2015

42 Show Your Face

It is difficult to express
the torment of this state
of anxious waiting
but I can try

Forms moving at a distance
look like you
Voices coming from afar
sound sweet like yours

I have grown used
to stepping out with hope
and turning back disheartened
I plan to fool you
by catching you off guard
but only get fooled myself

There is a brief respite
in trying to guess
what you might bring me

You might call
any minute
I have kept my cell phone
in my hand, on my chest
But
I keep checking
every few seconds
to see if I have missed your call

I keep checking
if I have 'silenced' it by mistake

I won't call you
It has to be you
If I call first
what's the point of this waiting?

Call
Show me your face
Come

I stand like an old woman
who waits for her grandson
to bring her the *karichoru**
he went to get

7 JUNE 2015

---

* *Karichoru*, in Tamil, refers to any kind of food (usually rice)
cooked with meat.

43 Protection

To escape
from the stray dogs chasing her
that female dog runs
and sits in front of the iron gate
of the house
that has dogs barking
from within

7 JUNE 2015

44 Your Visit

You visited
You made an impression
On your way out
you reached with your left hand
for the lush chilli plant out front
and plucked at it
Your visit
has become a memory

8 JUNE 2015

45 They Toil

My city
is filled with young people
It is a relief
they don't look anything
like our children

They wear clothes
that are good-looking, clean
and expensive
They wear backpacks
purchased online
to suit
the width of their backs

They only wear
attractive shoes
and good socks

They have learnt to eat
with spoons
elegantly, politely
without touching food with their hands

They have become
punctual
diligent
dutiful
employees

They toil
taking the night for the day
and the day for the night
leaping from night to day
and from day to night
and even forgetting
if it is night or day

May the world prosper

8 JUNE 2015

46 A Man of Culture

He needs some tea
He is a man of culture

He needs some tea
He gets up
pushing his chair backwards
a little too loudly
He bangs open
the bathroom door
and then slams it shut

He needs some tea
He walks all over the house
taking loud footsteps
He switches on the television
and turns the volume
higher than usual

He needs some tea
He goes into the kitchen
and upsets the vessels
and drinks some water
standing surrounded by the din
of falling metal

He needs some tea
But

he is a man of culture
His wife
has woken up from her nap

16 JUNE 2015

47 The Eraser

Using my body's moisture
I made an eraser

Clutching it in my hand
I started erasing
all my manuscripts
Little eraser curls fell into a pile
After many nights and days
the cleared pages
sparkled like lightning

I now stretch the eraser long
and use it like a brush on the wall
Everything, even the computer screen
regains its colour

Eraser starts dripping blood
I should keep erasing
even if it means smearing
everything with blood
Days, weeks
Months, years
I have pressed my eraser
against the wall of time

3 MAY 2015

48 What Shall I Do?

I have commanded my pen
that the ink-drip from its ball-tip
shall happen henceforth
only for signatures
accounts and
journal entries

Now
my signature varies
each time
It becomes serpentine curves
and brushstrokes
It refuses to stay within the box

When I look now
at yesterday's grocery accounts
I see the vegetables have come alive
There is a worm crawling in the rice

In a journal entry from two days ago
a one-legged crow has now appeared
and is sitting on the clothes line
Yesterday's entry has recorded
a barber's laments

Is my pen
disobeying my orders?
What can I do to it?

I am so angry
that I might break its tip
and fling it away

3 MAY 2015

49 Morality Alone Is Important

Morality alone is important, I say

Don't ask me
why, what for
Don't interrupt me
when I talk morality

I need no qualifications
to talk about morality
I need no special skills
to talk about morality

I will talk about morality everywhere
immorality is rampant
I will talk about morality to anyone
immorality is in everyone

I have great clarity about morality
I have even found out
where morality resides
I can talk about morality
for however long

I will let you in on a little secret
When I speak about morality
nipples
and vaginas
grow inside me

Even the tip of my penis
peeps out a little

17 JUNE 2015

50 Mere Grass

I didn't know
what happened to me
During my joyous walk
in the moonlight yesterday
I fell tripping on a blade of grass

'You trifling little blade of grass!' I yelled in anger
'We are trifling?' the blades of grass shrieked
Until that day I had not known
that grasses could speak
that their voices could come after you

I chided myself for my stupidity
ran into my house
bolted the door
and stayed within the walls

But at night
grasses held a meeting
spoke till they lost their voices
They decided to uproot themselves
and march and fast in protest

The words they had learnt
spread through their tips like poison

When I opened the door in the morning
there were grasses everywhere
their tips got into my nose

their blades curled up inside my ears
their edges scratched me everywhere

I lie covered in grass
I have never spat on the grass
I have never weeded them away
But
I lie covered in grass now

Grasses stand bold and tall
like trees
With no other choice, I say softly
'You are not mere leaves of grass
You are beautiful trees'

51 The Atheist

With the fervour and relish
of hurling
the worst insult at me
someone said
'You are an atheist'
'Yes
even
God knows
that'
I said

17 JUNE 2015

52 Old Accounts

Starting right from my drawing room
everywhere I ever set foot
I see people waiting
with old ledgers in hand

I did not know there could be
so many unsettled accounts
in my name
I didn't expect there would be
so many with books in hand

Some ledgers contain
just a single word I seem to have uttered
and forgotten at some point
The dues that grow from it
run to several pages

Some ledgers have registered
even the involuntary jerk
of my little finger
Pages growing from this
have spread out like the wind

Some have my laughter noted in the books
Some have my walk entered in the books
Some have my shirt noted in the books
Some have my voice entered in the books

My hair too is accounted for
prominently
Each of these
is a hardbound book
whose pages
you will never finish turning

On downward slopes
the weight of these old dues
presses down on my back
This is the burden of debts
secretly set down by hands
that held my feet up
on my climb upwards
I simply have to bear it

When the dues are not paid
knives will come out
Scratches and wounds
will become commonplace
cuts too
I just have to endure them

Thank you, Lord
for helping me see
how far back
my old debts go

9 MAY 2015

53 Starting Today

You carry
more than your hands can hold
It spills over from all sides
and on to the ground

How long can you hold on to it?
Won't it slip away through your fingers?
Won't the harsh sun just slurp it all up?
When your elbows hurt
you might jerk your hands
Time might produce its fungus

Why don't you extend your arms
towards expectant mouths?
You could offer these crow chicks
at least the drops that fall

Don't feign ignorance
and gaze at your feet
I will send my words
to be ants
in your ears

Here's proof number one:
Starting today
you won't digest
the food you eat

19 JUNE 2015

54 The Final Head

Fresh heads
roll at my feet
Fresh human heads
oozing warm blood

My face swells with pride
and I seem to grow bigger
each time a head falls
like a palmyra fruit cut down

Placing one foot on a head on the ground
and the other on a head high up on the pile
I stand looking up
sunlight forming a halo behind me

As per my orders
the severed heads
are rolled down to me
like shattered coconuts

I climb backwards
one step after another
on a staircase made of heads

Under my feet
heads
fresh heads
fresh human heads

But don't worry
On my hip I carry a sword
to chop off
the very last human head

12 MAY 2015

55 That Will Tell You

They refuse to believe
that I am dead
But death is only natural
People grow old and die
People get sick and die
People die in accidents
in floods, in earthquakes
from cold, from heat
Murders and
suicides abound

My death
is just one among these
Call it mass murder
or a coward's suicide
Call it drama
Call it even a lie
a trick, a pretence

Once you are done naming it
go about your daily business
I will clear away the darkness
of the moment of my death
turn it into a star
and fix it on the sky
That will speak
forever and ever

19 JUNE 2015

56 The Sea's Silence

Wherever I go people ask
the same question in different ways
'Has the sea fallen silent?'

Those who know the sea
those who have seen the sea
those who have seen images of the sea
those who have neither seen nor known
but heard of the sea
All have just one thing to ask
'Has the sea fallen silent'?

'The sea has fallen silent,' I tell them
Can it? Can it?
Can it fall silent?
Can the sea fall silent?

But the sea has indeed gone quiet
Silence on its surface
and the tumult of waves in the deep

19 JUNE 2015

57 The Butcher

That day I saw from up close
the strength of a butcher's actions

The goat was tied
to an iron pole
Sprig hung on a long rope
close to its mouth
The goat went about its business
pulling leaves from the sprig
by its front teeth
bleating a little
waving its tail
walking around the pole

In its eyes
a little terror, or sorrow, or confusion
It could be from thirst
or from the new surroundings
or from the flow of customers

The butcher
paid no attention to the goat

He chopped meat into bits
knowing well
what force to use for which part
His knife scraped and cleaned
the grease spread
on the wooden cutting board

Suddenly
he untied the goat
pushed it down
pressed his foot on its vocal chord
and cut its throat
with his chopper

The beauty of a white flower
unfolding, blushing

He caught without wasting
the gush of sweet blood drops
in a vessel
He paid no attention
to the body that shuddered
and fell silent

I have endless affection
for the butcher
I am his fan
Butchery is the greatest art

I can spend the rest of my life
watching a goat's throat being cut
or
stepping on its neck
and taking my chopper to it

13 MAY 2015

58 Breathing Exercises

As usual
I am walking
on the left side of the road
ruminating
on the moments I had lost
when I was dead
On the memories
of sorrow trampling on me
On the wonders
of the lives of ancestors
I am walking
like a goat relishing the shade

The present and the future
gently come and go
like a cradle rocked by the wind

As usual
I let out a few sighs
The police appear
out of nowhere
and surround me

It seems there was a complaint
that my breath blared
like a fire truck's siren
Could such a wail have emerged
from a sigh even I couldn't hear?
Really? Really? I ask

They warn me, they threaten me
Arrest, jail time
it is all possible, they say
I express remorse
I ask for forgiveness

They let me walk
but keep watch over me
Holding my breath in as long as I can
I reach my room
I shut all doors and windows
and risk breathing a little
I even try sighing
It sounds like a needle falling
Perhaps it is too loud

If the sound of my breathing spills out
it might bruise someone's ears
Reaching in through their ears
it might wound their hearts

Be it the past
the present or
the future
from now on
I shall not sigh over anything
It might be good if I can hold in
even my shallow breath
I shouldn't hurt anyone

I learn to breathe
slowly

very slowly
trying not to move even the hair in my nostrils
I learn to breathe
slowly
very slowly

I learn to breathe
steadily
very steadily
without disturbing
even a flower petal
I learn to breathe
steadily
very steadily

It is certainly difficult
but
breathing exercises are necessary
breathing exercises are good for us

20 JUNE 2015

59 The Howls

Piercing through
the dense midnight dark
that had dry leaves for eyes
came a rabid dog

No one knew
where it came from
or who had sent it

Those who heard
the language of its bark
reckoned it was
an enemy conspiracy
Others said
that it was the pet dog
of an evil, vengeful man

Some even said
it was the pharmacist's ploy
to sell long-stocked medicine
A few also said
it was the king's message
meant to turn his subjects
into echoes of a single ruling voice

No one knew for sure
where it came from
or who had sent it

The rabid dog entered
with its drooling tongue
touching the ground

Street dogs barked at it
but it moved unfazed
It turned suddenly
bit one of the dogs
and ran
Street dogs pounced on it
But in the middle of this big fight
the rabid dog hid itself
where no one could find it

After a silence of a few days
dogs that bit and
dogs that were bitten
roamed around with their drooling tongues out
Barks became howls
They bit the chickens
that raked about in the trash out front
They bit the goats
that went about chewing dry grass
They bit the cows
whose lives went as far as the ropes did
They bit the house dogs
when they went outside to shit
The howls resounded everywhere

Men grew fearful
Those who ventured out

curious to know the conditions
rushed back in with bloody wounds

After a silence of a few days
one person bit another
another bit yet another
yet another bit still another
still another bit the next person
the next person bit the next
the next person bit the next
thus the scene unfolded

Drooling tongues
Howls
Packs of rabid dogs

21 JUNE 2015

60 Come Quietly

Resistance
Revolution
Mutiny
These are all
worthless words today

All that is left
is to die, flesh torn
and ravaged, like a chicken
caught among crows

I ask for nothing, sir
Let me just live
as a spectator
as a mere spectator

How can that be?
How could we bear
the condescending smile
of a teetotaller
in this drunken revelry?

Even the dirt in your fingertips
will be noticed
made much of
Daggers will unite
to chop off the finger

If you resist, you will vanish
If you keep aloof, you will be ruined
Swindling, fraud
murder, selfishness
robbery, jealousy
are all part of the game

There is only one way from here on

Just come quietly
partake in all of this
You will prosper

14 MAY 2015

61 I Didn't Learn a Thing

I didn't learn a thing
from my colleague
who sat right next to me at work

He was ready to teach me everything
He gestured to me many times
to simply follow him
but I declined without even a consideration

He was my senior in the office
'No need to do any work
If necessary, we can pretend to be working
We need to be cordial to everyone
Be ready to lick anyone's feet'
These were the mottos he imparted to me

Those who do nothing
face no problems
Unambitious people get to enjoy life

When it came out in the open
that he misbehaved with a woman
the union rushed to his rescue
He had never taken part
in protests, fasts
slogans or strikes
But he paid his membership dues diligently
A 'silent member'

After work, he'd head straight home
and roam like a pet dog
within the outer walls
There was a little garden there
that one couldn't see from outside
No one knew what grew there
But you could see his head
when he hung about in the garden

House, car, cash
children, education
He wanted for nothing
Ration card, PAN card
Voter ID card, driving licence
ATM card
(from three banks, as far as I know)
Mediclaim card
ID card
(he'd change the photo now and then)

He was meticulous
He knew all the expiry dates
but he'd still check everything
on the first of every month
He'd update things tirelessly
change even the smallest details
Voter ID alone
he corrected twenty times
He'd even say that his card
was the only correct one in the country

He was the first one in our town
to get an Aadhaar card
He said that they issued them then
only in the post office
He paid his electricity bill on time
and reminded me after the due date
He was the first one to receive
any notification
that the state sent out to its citizens
He never ever failed to pay
any tax, any fee on time

Children's weddings, grandsons and granddaughters
pension, going for a walk twice a day
a full medical check-up once a month

A full life

I didn't learn anything from him
He was willing to be my guru and show me the way
But
I let go of the chance
to be a model citizen

14 MAY 2015

62 Poetic Subject

My gaze falls anew
on nature

Nature is the last refuge
for one who has lost everything
has nothing and
is dead

Like a lover
it embraces with open arms
the one who worships it
Like the mother of an errant child
it caresses with pride
the one who slanders it

My naked mind lets go
and descends
to inhale nature's scent
to drink of its many hues
to bathe in its life spring

My mind will
hold on to raindrops
and surge skywards
leap on lush trees
climb their branches
roll like a pig over the hillsides
An eternal spring in its step
A perpetual joy

Yes
Time
asks me to make
my poetic subject
pure nature
that knows
no human scent

13 MAY 2015

63 The Sky

A motorbike racer crosses
in a flash
the road I haven't managed to cross
on foot or
on my vehicles
in all these years

He is also the one who fell
spreading out his wings
from on top of the bridge

How will I console
his parents
who rely on him?
What words do I have
for his lover who whimpers
hiding her heart
reluctant to show her face?

Among people
who remain mere spectators
despite the desire to learn to fly
he was one who actually flew
Even now
he is out there flying somewhere
The sky is only for the winged

5 JULY 2015

64 My Only Answer

What hereafter
What before
What now
What
What what
What what what
To all these
inquisitive whats
my only answer is

Nothing

14 MAY 2015

65 Immaculate

I am immaculate
and so is my wife

My father was immaculate
and so was my mother

My grandfather was immaculate
as was my grandmother

My great-grandfather was immaculate
My great-grandmother too

My great-grandfather's father's father and his wife
He and his wife
and he and his wife

Why
My entire lineage
which knows
only its chastity belt
is immaculate

14 MAY 2015

66 An Easy Task

for Kalburgi

Killing
is the easiest of tasks

You don't have to hide
from the eyes of the murdered
The dead body will not catch
your scent
Its blue tongue and dry lips
will not shed
a single word against you
There is no way it can hear
the emptiness
in your fiery uproar
There is no chance it can raise
even a finger against you

Argument and counter-argument
writing and art
history and conflict
unity and difference
research and literature
war and peace
are useless pursuits
The simplest of jobs
is to kill
Corpses do not think

31 AUGUST 2015

67 Bitterness

Even though
I am fond of bitterness
I hadn't experienced much of it
Only the bitterness
of cooked bitter gourd

Early one dawn, with my mind gone bitter
I plucked and ate a handful
of tender neem shoots
Bitter mouth, bitter tongue
bitter saliva, bitter voice
I slowly chewed on the bitterness

An elder in a loincloth
appeared in my path
and told me I could counter
even snake venom
if I ate neem leaves every day

Every day now
I eat a whole neem tree
Nothing short
of turning my whole body bitter
would do
These are times
when the very air is venomous

14 MAY 2015

68 Recognition

By enemy conspiracy
or kin's ploy
the king lost his kingdom
and wandered like a nomad

The loss of luxury didn't bother him
He slept happily and alone outdoors
getting to know the trees
looking at the sky
meeting people
seeing crores and crores of living things

When he saw with a little pride
that there was no hunger
in his kingdom
that it was filled with rest houses
free food, water shelters
welcoming homes and hospitality
he let his mind wander
in the star-studded sky

When he delighted swimming in the rivers
When he enjoyed walking in the fields
When he roamed around
among revelrous festival crowds
When he made himself seem a mendicant
with his beard and moustache
he still wanted

no, he waited, yearning
for only one thing

Won't some eyes—
even if they were to be his enemies'—
recognize him
as the one who once ruled?

5 SEPTEMBER 2015

69 Here

Here
things I like are but a few
things I don't like abound

For the rare chance
of getting what I like
I struggle all the time
with what I don't like

This world that is filled with what I don't like
is not mine
It is in the effort to create my world
that I spend my life

23 SEPTEMBER 2015

70 The White Crow

It was born
to crow parents
from crow eggs
in a crow's nest
as a crow baby

It lived
as a crow
eating as a crow
cawing as a crow
flying around as a crow

On the edges of the crow's ashen feathers
was a little streak of white
that the other crows frowned upon
A lime stain on crow feathers, they thought
The crows tried to brush it away lovingly
The crows rubbed at the stain
chiding the young crow affectionately
The crows got mad at it
and made it take a bath

The white spread on the crow's feathers
The crow slowly turned white
The crow became a white crow
The crows started saying
that the white crow had a disease
The crows went around saying
that the white crow didn't have
a crow mind

The white crow's spit
doesn't look like a crow's, said one
The white crow's caw
doesn't sound like a crow's, said one
The white crow's neck
doesn't turn like a crow's, said one
The white crow simply
doesn't look like a crow, said one

From the crow family
but with a crane's hue
What could the white crow do?
It thought of dying
falling headlong from a peak
but couldn't find the courage
It sat alone on trees
flew alone in the sky
ate alone
laughed alone
cried alone
it lived alone, alone

All crows
looked in wonder
at the white crow
But the white crow
looked in wonder
at the whole world

24 SEPTEMBER 2015

71 I Am One of You

I admit I am a little old-fashioned

Yesterday, I made someone trip and fall
His teeth shattered and bloodied his face
Though I did it deliberately
I still lost some sleep over it

The night before, I strangled someone
Like a goat caught under a butcher's foot
he uttered a deep-throated cry
I relished killing him
but there is still some blood
seeping through my fingers

Today
with many ideas
I am stalking a woman
but I feel a bit hesitant

I realize now
that I am a little old-fashioned
But don't worry
if I get over this little snag
I am fully one of you

23 SEPTEMBER 2015

72 Pavayi

My grandmother's name was Pavayi
Her family called her 'Pavu'
'Eley!' was how my grandfather addressed her
She called him by her eldest daughter's—
that is, my paternal aunt's—name
She'd raise her voice
and call out, 'Ponna! Ponna!'

She'd roam around the fields
with breasts sagging
much like the pouch dangling from her hip
She'd always carry a knife
and a sickle on her waist

The eldest granddaughter—
that is, my younger sister—
was named after her

Once when she was twenty-eight
my sister stood in line at a bank
(it was a busy day at the bank)
and they called out, 'Pavayi! Pavayi!'

When she returned home
she cried and she cried
and cried some more
No one cried that much
even when my grandmother died

73 The Execution Hall

I like moonlight
Therefore
I created an execution hall
on a full moon night
After all, I do need some light
to pick the faces to kill

Now
I am the supervisor of the execution hall
My initial misgivings
have slowly gone away

What does a supervisor do?
In the early part of the night, I pick the faces

Appearances I don't like
Gazes I don't like
Characters I don't like
Gestures I don't like
Politics I don't like
Caste I don't like
Religion I don't like
Authority I don't like
Places I don't like

Good lord!
There is so much I don't like
Rather than saying, 'things I don't like'
you could say, 'things I didn't get'

I am also the one
who chooses the appropriate method
of execution
Since I basically consider this a war
I mostly use the traditional sword

A butcher's knife for throat slitters
A cross-hilted dagger for backstabbers
A short sword for traitors
A serrated knife for snitches
A bullet for the petty
Explosions too are used to kill them all at once

What does an execution chamber's supervisor do?
That is, besides going to sleep peacefully
after counting the heads at dawn

6 SEPTEMBER 2015

74 So Many, So Many

So far
so many days
so many nights
on this earth

From those
each life
took up
so many nights
so many days

Still
so many nights
so many days
left
on this earth

Among those
so many nights
so many days
left
for each life

My life has seen
so many nights
so many days
in this world

Still
so many nights
so many days
left for me

Among those
so many nights
so many days
that I will cross
that need to be crossed
that shall never be crossed

They are all the same
but also
each a little different

15 MAY 2015

75 Cloud Waterfall

In the rainy season
when I climb down a steep slope
and look up
the waterfall is in spate
looking like clouds have torn open the sky
come down
and draped themselves over the rocks

I become a single drop of water
and blend in

In summer
the dark rock looks like a giant honeycomb
and the thinned waterfall hangs
like a lone aerial root

I look up
mouth agape in wonder
my hair dry and tangled

Everything
should be seen twice
says the cloud waterfall

16 MAY 2015

76 The Alternative

A thousand people got together
and moved a tree
They said it was a poisonous tree
The tree that had stood firmly clutching the earth
had to slacken its hold
It rose slowly, moved its branches
kicked its feet and started flying
blessing
the gods that taught it how to fly

1 OCTOBER 2015

77 That One Day

There is one day
one specific day
in your life
that you can never forget
The day you were killed
in front of your eyes

1 OCTOBER 2015

78 Clarity

Eternal confusion
Occasional clarity

Like a sliver of moon
breaking free of cloud cover
here's some clarity I found today:
hands that forsake
never were
hands that held

1 OCTOBER 2015

79 War

This is certainly war
Weapons in all hands
Facing them stands
unarmed
silence.

4 OCTOBER 2015

80 Great Souls

Great souls come to me
I run into great souls
Great souls invite me
Great souls talk to me

One of them stays silent
One of them smiles a little
One of them is sad
One of them sheds tears

Some words come to me directly
Some words flit past my ears
Some words sound delighted
Some words are sizing me up

Great souls take leave slowly
Great souls bid farewell
Great souls make an impression
Great souls vanish without a trace

Until not long ago
I too
was a great soul

1 MAY 2015

81 Unleashed

Speak, speak, they tell me
I am simply wandering
in a wordless dawn

Tell us, tell us, they say
I am just roaming around
in a forest where
no questions arise
no answers are needed

Write, write, they tell me
I am swinging freely
on the edge of a pristine world
unconquered yet by writing

I am a creature broken free of its leash
Let me meander through lost time

4 OCTOBER 2015

82 Each to Their Own

Yielding to my tongue and stomach
I reached up to pluck
at the branch of the drumstick tree
It snapped and fell
with flowers and tender little drumsticks
Its wail lasted a second

When I walked fast
wearing branded footwear
ants and other insects
got crushed underfoot
Not a sound

Loud voices of passers-by
jolted awake
a child that was sleeping
after a long lullaby
A loud bawl

Each with their own goal
Each on their own path
There is nothing we can do

17 MAY 2015

83 I Like the Rainy Season Too

I have returned home
like the hero of Sangam poems
who leaves in the summer
and returns with the rains

I wipe away my wife's tears
who waits for me at the doorstep
I think of my mother
who has passed away not long ago
I turn the time between
summer and monsoon
into a story for my children
Relatives
come and go freely

It rains
I close the curtains
and enjoy
the cold nights
I poison and kill the insects
that come seeking refuge
It's an uneventful time

I wipe things clean
I keep wiping
to keep fungus away
I look for blotches of seepage on the walls
and seal them
There are several leaks

I keep plugging them

Day dawns
Day ends

It rains
Now and then I part the curtains
and look outside
Lightning darts across the sky
I hear thunder

They say the weather will change
But I tell them
I like the rainy season
One can just stay in when it rains

17 MAY 2015

84 What Can I Possibly Do?

What can I possibly do?

I am the lowest average
whose life spins around
work, family, sleep
savings, identity cards

What can I possibly do?

I am a citizen
who gets
his bureaucratic transactions done
without standing in lines for too long
without running from pillar to post
thanks to the kindness, to the references
of old classmates, friends
friends of friends
relatives, acquaintances

What can I possibly do?

I don't ask for too much
Only a chair under the ceiling fan
at work during summer
and an hour's leeway
when it rains

What can I possibly do?

Newspapers
television news channels
debates
goat-herding
political conversations
I have the knack
of agreeing, smiling
without taking sides
on any of these

I have never told anyone
which party
I vote for

My struggle is to hold on
to what I get
I am the kind who floats
on a piece of driftwood
holding my head above
the water

What can I possibly do?

Other than feigning
ignorance
when I actually know
everything
what can I
possibly do?

What can I possibly do?

18 MAY 2015

85 Just One Request

When did my running start?
At dark?
At the light of dawn?
During the scorching midday heat?
During the comfort of dusk?
Does anyone know?
Why am I still running?
What is chasing me?
A dog disturbed?
A ghost awakened?
Are these just hallucinations?
Just hallucinations?
Can my feet keep up
with a formless illusion?

How far should I run?
For all my life?
Till the end of the world?
Will the chase ever end?
Are there no answers?
May I request just one thing?
Just one?
May I stop for just a second
to catch my breath?

13 OCTOBER 2015

86 Alms

My words have dried up
Usually, when I give birth to them
they take their first step
out into the world
with the wet stickiness
of a newborn

Those days are now a faded memory
Now I anxiously spit on my words
to make them wet
I touch and fondle them with my fingers
I make my spit their identity

When nothing works
I beg you
for your spit
You are generous souls, aren't you?

13 OCTOBER 2015

87 Motives

Motives
generous motives
narrow motives
secret motives
frank motives
motive within motive
motive without motive

You made me see everything
by making me step
on a single trap

I bow to you
my lord

18 MAY 2015

88 Becoming

I have been looking at the rain
for three days now

Drizzle, sprinkle
a soft whine
moderate, steady force
heavy downpour
silence

Succour for lives that stand thirsty
mouths open

The waters flow into
a large pond
a long river
a vast ocean

All I need to do
is become a drop of rain
I can fall from the sky
and reach the sea

18 MAY 2015

89 Taking Aim

The town has become a city
but it is still a town in some ways
Immigrant ghosts
have mingled
with native ghosts
and hang upside down in buildings

Streets have narrowed
Crowds have grown
and they run everywhere
bloodthirsty tongues hanging out
Peace, sympathy
grace, compassion
love
everything's been deemed unmarketable
and thrown in the gutter

Human heads are up for sale
There are schools that teach
how to make heads roll
There are agents to decide
how much heads are worth

Anybody's head
can roll any time
Time goes by
in touching one's head

from time to time
while taking aim at others'

18 MAY 2015

90 Forest Feast 1

for C. Chandran

You took me to a forest
Bees welcomed us, buzzing
sprinkling scented water

There were trees I couldn't recognize
that looked exactly
like the trees I could recognize
Plants, creepers, insects
little creatures

I tried to identify them
with names I knew
names I tried
to prove right
but failed

More and more disappointments
I rejoiced at the sight
of a large mango tree
It was definitely a mango tree
no doubt
You gave me a ripe, fallen fruit
I bit into it eagerly
thinking it was a Neelam fruit
Sourness
A sourness as if all of the world's sourness
had been rolled into one

The forest has preserved the originals
We are busy celebrating fakes

20 MAY 2015

91 Forest Feast 2

for Sasi

Like an unyielding creeper
that ascends
grabbing on to the rough surface
of a tree
we climbed higher and higher
along the path of a wild river
stepping
from one rock to another
holding on
to one rock and leaping
on to another

Various sights and scenes
along the waterway
Getting drenched by the little waterfall
A moment in its rush
as it sped through a crevice
Bathing, lying on the water
as it spread on the rocks
Half-heartedly
and with some threats
the water revealed its every secret
Slowly we learnt to climb
holding on to the water

We will strive a little more
to learn

to move through water
to learn
to dwell inside water

20 MAY 2015

92 Forest Feast 3

for Samiyaar Sathiyavel

In the middle of the forest
Periyasami, the god
and Kannimar, the virgin goddesses
have claimed their separate spots
under the ghost tree
on top of the large rock

I asked you if you were scared
You said you had the spear
Three or four rusted spears
stood affixed to the ground
in front of us

In the forest
there is no feud
over territories
and borders
But I still asked you
who owned how much
You replied that
if one went right
the other went left
That it is all theirs

Vermilion, flowers, fruits, camphor
a closed lamp-cage lay about

all left by the humans
who come up the hill

Humans do their best
to make a beggar out of anyone
Why should this be an exception?

The polythene bag that hangs
from the trident is the collection box
Like a dog's milk-filled teats
it hangs swollen and full
with coins

Does no one take out the money?
was my predictable question

They only put in money
they never take out
they are afraid to
you said

Periyasami and Kannimar too
don't touch the money
In the forest
it amounts to nothing
it is like dirt

21 MAY 2015

93 Forest Feast 4

for Gopi

We saw the wondrous canal
the divine mason had carved
on a rock
A torrential rush of water
suddenly streams itself
into the canal
and flows within its bounds
but at great speed
It swells with frothy waves
and glides down the canal

The water sloshes and falls
into a demon's cupped hands
It also brings down a bundle of clouds
and blows a gust of wind from above

Overcome with the desire
to float and slide on the water
you suddenly lie down
on the canal
The foam closes in on you
and you vanish
Then I see a shimmer
It could be a rock
or your body
I see you pulled along

by the water
For a short while
you become water

21 MAY 2015

94 Forest Feast 5

for Yuvaraj

The forest and the waterfall
welcome us with open arms
but you hesitate to shed your clothes

These humans
have crammed your head with many such things
things you are loath to let go of
You should be ready to shed the thorns in just one shake

You curve your palm into a cup
point to the water that fills and flows out of it
and say this much is enough to run a house
Then you say that twice as much water
is enough to irrigate three acres of land

But this is life in the wild
It starts in the forest
flows in the forest
ends in the forest

You can have this forest life
if you can let go of everything else
Otherwise
even your memory would imprison you

21 MAY 2015

95 In My Dream

Let's talk
I tell those who come to kill me
in my dream
And they agree

2 NOVEMBER 2015

96 The End

There isn't much time left
Everything needs to be resolved
Everything needs to come to an end

Will it be by water
or fire?

Our only hope
is an earthquake

Nature will take care of it

18 MAY 2015

97 I Won't Talk

How many words
does your gargantuan appetite need?

I gave you fortified words
You spat them out
saying they were teeth-shattering
they wouldn't digest

I gave you words filled with wellness
You chewed them to pulp
added your spittle
and spat them back right at me
It stinks, it stinks
you proclaimed to the wind

I gave you words of supplication
In a single burp, you swallowed
a slave's shrunken form
and asked for more and more

You took away everything from me
I now show you
a lap bereft of words
Please leave me

5 NOVEMBER 2015

98 Discoveries

I have lived in this city for long
I have learnt a lot about it
I could call them my discoveries

It was only by chance
that I discovered the roadside stall
run by a family that sells
idli, chutney, dosa and sambar
cooked homestyle

The man who sells
old-style *kuzhai puttu* on a pushcart
stops in a different street every day
It took some effort to find out
that he was one of a kind and
on which street he stops
on which day

The electrician who not only comes
as soon as called
but also speaks with concern
The courier boy who was upset
I didn't tell him grandma was sick
The man who buys old newspapers
who smiles when he passes me by
on the street
Chintamaniyamma who comes every six months
and makes the toilet sparkle
The old man who looks at my beard

and says, 'Shall I cut the grass?'
The only shop on the lane that sells herbal powders
The Gandhi Ashram branch
where you can get neem tooth powder
Anbazhagan who cuts my hair neatly
without turning my head too often

I am leaving all of this
for a different city
I will have to discover
everything anew there
New discoveries
It will be exciting
for sure

21 MAY 2015

142

99 No Hurry

Annoyed
you kick and kick
trying to start the vehicle
that refuses to budge

The vehicle
knows
it is no one's mount

I am looking
at your urgency
your agitation
But
I am in no hurry

5 NOVEMBER 2015

I know my seasons
Summer with its long days
is a storehouse of compassion
Monsoon with its clouds
is love's wet kiss
My winter is the shiver of blessing
that sits on the tips of grass
Now
there is a mist falling
that will singe everything

101 Don't Chase It Away

The hen
bears the embryo
picks a spot
and lays its eggs patiently
If it adds its body's warmth
connects to the lives within
and waits for a few days
a little stirring
Taking form and breaking the shell
the little ones will emerge
with their cotton-soft feathers

But you extend your cruel hands
and gather the eggs away

Its brooding frenzy unfinished
the hen gathers stones
and sits on them
thinking they are eggs

Don't chase it away
at least now
They might be just stones for you
But they are eggs for the hen

5 NOVEMBER 2015

102 I Too Know about Pigs

for Kuvalaikkannan

I knew about pig's meat
long before I ever saw a pig
Its well-cooked skin
feels great on the teeth
like a piece of coconut

We kept strained pig fat
at home
We used it to treat cows
and to keep insects away

We bought dried pig shit
carried it in a cart
and used it as manure
Everything grew well
especially the chilli plant

Pigs are fat
They breed like crazy
They eat shit
They wallow in the muck
Therefore
when we wish to insult someone
we call them a pig

But none of this
turned into an affection for pigs

It was only when my little daughter
grew fond of the pigs she saw
on her way to school
and insisted I caught one for her
that I became fond of pigs
I started noticing them

The lovely sight of piglets running around
like keyed dolls
The way they compete
to feed at their mother's udders

Pigs too are beautiful
when they are young

22 MAY 2015

103 The Faceless Ones

The people who come in my dream threaten me
None of them has a face
My days are wasted away
in trying to identify faceless people

Even the ones I meet in the day are faceless
I fail to understand
How those without eyes see
How those without noses smell
How those without mouths consume
How those without ears hear
How those without faces function

I talk to the faceless
looking for their faces
I walk with the faceless
searching for their faces
I live with the faceless
staring at their faces
It lasts just seconds

Faceless people
are terrified of my face
Faceless people
run away from my face
Faceless people
spread many rumours about my face
Newsreaders announce that
my forehead is a fertile field of harm

my eyes are firebrands
my nose is a scorpion sting
my mouth a field of riots
my ears the hooks of destruction

I can see my face in the mirror
the face that the faceless hate
Why do I need a face to live among the faceless?
They scratch my face with their nails
Now it is a face of scratches
They tear up my face with knives
Now it is a bloodied face
They torch my face
Now it is a charred face
They punch my face with their fists
Now it is a swollen face

Why do I need a face to live among the faceless?
I get that
But what I don't know
is what I need to do
to become one among the faceless

23 MAY 2015

104 New Doors

I close
all doors
still my body
like a corpse
and simply watch
the rain

A black drongo
enters the hut
for refuge

In the movement
of its forked tail
new doors
keep opening
one after another

24 MAY 2015

105   A New Language

In one single day
I exhausted
the treasure trove of words
I had gathered all my life

With all the talking
and all the telling

How often can I repair
worn-out things?
How many times can I seal
the leaks?

I toss
my language
in the trash

Hereafter
a new language
Silence

25 MAY 2015

106 A Satisfying Death

I witnessed
my own death

I experienced
no pleasure or pain

I sensed a giant bird
spread its wings
and take off
I saw the dust storm
from the bird's flight
lift and fling away people

I saw the bird surge up
and darken the day sky
before vanishing
Then
like a summer's dawn
the sky appeared clean and bright

25 MAY 2015

107 Question and Answer

They point their fingers at him
demanding answers
All that they pose as questions
are, in fact, answers
prepared in advance

All he has are questions
questions that look like answers
His answer becomes a question
His question becomes an answer

Question question
answer answer
question answer
answer question
answer answer
question question

Are there answers?
It is all just questions, isn't it?

27 MAY 2015

My country My city
My village My home
My land My well
My tree My plant

My mother My father
My lover My wife
My daughter My son
My people My relations

My pen My book
My clothes My jewels
My place My object
My job My duty

My authority My victory
My language My writing
My story My song
My brain My mind

My hand My sign
My day My week
My year My life
My thought My donkey

My opinion My dog
My value My respect
My religion My caste

My race My clan
My hair My lump of clay

Remove the 'My'
from each of these
Mere words

28 MAY 2015

109   A Single Twig

I have found out
what I need to do

Politicians, officers
relatives, friends
colleagues
people on the streets
elites and commoners
Everyone
is afflicted with one thing
which is easy to cure
Very easy, very, very easy

I have gathered like twigs
every single word of praise there is
and kept them with me
tied like a bundle of firewood
I draw each from the bundle
and aim it
at the right person
at the right time

No matter how big the person
no matter how majestic
a single twig brings them down

It has to be a direct attack
There can be no hesitation

If you spot anything like
sarcasm
criticism
mockery
in my speech
don't, simply don't
tolerate it
or plot revenge
or let it fester

Just
hit me right away
with your shoes

29 MAY 2015

110   A Blank Page

In my dream
I am writing an exam

The entire exam
is nothing but
blanks to fill

In truth, they are not really questions
They are sentences to test memory
They are arrows aimed at experience
demanding recollection
They are dark lines that hide answers
that someone has decided already

I try to pry open the blanks
looking for answers
I press forcefully along some of the lines
When I turn the page
I find nothing but lines everywhere
Not even the reverse imprint of words

Just when I break into a sweat
afraid that I might have to turn in
a blank page
I wake up

31 MAY 2015

111 Company

The engineers who have fixed
exhaust fans
in apartment bathrooms
are kind souls

Pigeons roost
in these circular holes
They lay eggs, incubate
hatch their chicks, raise them
When one leaves the spot
another pigeon takes over

It becomes scared
when you enter the bathroom
Sometimes it flies away
But if you get used
to each other's sounds
and grow comfortable
you might get to look at the pigeon
with love
the pigeon might look at you
with affection

Don't feel shy
when you find the pigeon
poking its beak
through a gap
in the exhaust fan's cage

and looking at your nakedness
After all, the pigeon
is all the company you have left

31 MAY 2015

112 Wonders

They are all
wonders of creation

In my town
there is someone
with ears like leaves
Ears that spread out wide
like castor bean leaves

Those ears can absorb
even the whispers
in the vicinity
They can take in
even the chatter
from far away

All those who went with serrated knives
to chop off the ears
returned with worshipful reverence
once they got to savour a few pus-drops
of what the ears had gathered

In my town
there is someone
with a nose like a capsicum
Large and swollen

It'd put a bloodhound to shame
It can tell apart

the fragrances in the air
It can quickly point
to washed and unwashed bodies
to bodies smelling of last night's sex
Those who went with a knife
to cut off the nose
came back after praying to it
enchanted by its incense

In my town
there is someone
with eyes of fire
They are awake and aflame
like a fire made on a winter night

They wander everywhere
and capture scenes no one has seen
They are wonderfully adept
at capturing who was with whom
when, where
and for how long

Those who went with spears
to gouge out these eyes
were lulled by its pornography
and sang paeans to it

In my town
there is someone
with a muscled body
that could withdraw at a touch
like a snail into its shell

A finger or a needle or a twig
it shivers before it is even touched
With its sensor-like hairs
it stays permanently alert

Those who went with needles
to drag it out of its shell
end up hailing
the strength of its armour

In my town
there is someone
with a small mouth
A mouth that shrinks and expands
like an anus

When it opens a little
it passes wind quietly
If it opens wider
it farts loudly
It can open variously
and even shit

Those who couldn't bear the stench
and went with scissors
to cut off the lips
lay on their backs
submerged, entranced
by the sight of maggots
squirming in the shit

They are all
wonders of creation

in my town
Which one is mine?
Perhaps the wondrous mind
that can spot wonders?

11 JUNE 2015

113   All at Once

A minor storm
has destroyed everything
Trees stand with their branches torn apart
Birds with ripped wings
writhe and struggle on the ground
There is a stench of dog corpses everywhere
Light spreads over everything
like a white shroud
Having lost
all its love all at once
my gaze squirms like a worm in the gutter

12 JUNE 2015

In a forest
where no one could tell the directions
the wild pig lived a charmed life
since no one could tell when
it bathed in the stream, drank clean water
smelt the fresh soil
ate roots and tubers
slept peacefully in the shade of dense bushes
roamed around with its crowd
made love and made piglets
and won the battle of survival

A hunter caught in a net
two of the piglets that were playing
over a wild jasmine creeper
and took them to his village
His wife grew fond of the newborns
fed them milk, became their mother
Away from the forest, among people
the pig family grew and thrived

The tamed pig now spends its day
in the village
where everyone can tell directions
It bathes in the sewer, drinks from drainage
smells shit
pokes around and eats ashes
sleeps in a thatched enclosure

mates and yields piglets
and gets sacrificed for meat

The wild pig will never know the village
The country pig will never know the forest

13 JUNE 2015

115   Prayer

Enough Enough
You have given enough, enough
Enough Enough
You have taken enough, enough
Enough Enough
Leave what is left
Leave a little
Leave me be
Leave Leave
Just let me go
Leave
Enough Enough
It is all enough
Po dhum Po dhum
E nough E nough
E nough
E
nough
Po dhum Po dhum
Po
dhum
Go Go
Po Po
dhum dhum dhum
dhum dhum dhum
dhum
m

mm
mmm

13 JUNE 2015

116   Speak

Speak whatever you want

Theism, atheism
caste, religion
community, language
god, animal
farmer, worker
government, party, leader
environment, terrorism
organic farming
black money, election
literature, arts, music
research, science
position, responsibility
whatever

Speak whatever you want

But
speak
my word

13 JUNE 2015

117 Twice, Thrice

Yesterday's
objects of affection
have gone jaded today
I've grown weary of affection itself
The intervals
in my daily work calendar
have become the allotted times for affection
I panic when I run out of them
so I top them up
now and then

I haven't been able
to dismiss affection completely
The alternative
is emptiness

Affection has become a habit
like brushing one's teeth
every day
Some days
I brush twice or thrice

14 JUNE 2015

118   Little Birds

I try to scrub away the rust
formed over the memories
of my childhood playtime
I forge ahead
hanging on to the little glimmer
that I see under my scratch

A little garden with
a thick shrub of crossandra flowers
a vine of grapes
a single coconut tree
the squeals of squirrels
the crows that come on time
the frog that calls from the little well
And amidst them all
little footprints
soft little feet
soft little hands
soft little mouths
soft little bodies
soft little laughter
and everywhere
soft little flames

I've plucked and taken to my heart
one of those flames
And I am coming to see you
today

14 JUNE 2015

119 The Calendar

When I turn on the fan
the pages of the calendar
flutter

It struggles
months scrambled
days confused
but
the sound of its very being
wipes away my sweat
cleanses me
comforts me

When its rustling
turns to pestering
I sit in front of it
and open the day
it has offered me

It calms down slowly
sits like a schoolkid
arms folded across the chest
a finger on the lips
The calendar looks, listens
and settles into meditation

15 JUNE 2015

120 The Big Child

A child needs more than a toy
to play with
It also needs another child
In a city house
with just the first child
or
the only child
the father or the mother
grandfather, grandmother, ayah, servant, guest
someone
becomes the other child

And the two children play
rolling a ball
driving a car
spreading and arranging toys
flinging them about
running around

After a while
the small child
goes to sleep on the floor
But the big child
plays alone
happily

15 JUNE 2015

121 Your Room

I have not seen
your room
This is what I surmise
from what you have told me

It is neither
on the earth
nor on the sky
It hangs in between

It has no doors
or windows
Only walls

I make no assumptions
about the things
it contains
They might be things I don't know

Not only I
no other friend or relative
has ever entered
your room
You have invited no one
It makes you anxious
when someone
wants to visit you

You don't like people's suggestions
You don't like redecorating

You move through it
like a breeze

Do you really have
a room
of your own?

16 JUNE 2015

122   The Way They Came In

When we moved into the apartment building
ants moved in with us
Then a little later came
cockroaches and crickets

Some keep fish
Some have dogs
Then there is the cry from below
of cats that don't climb the stairs

Pigeons and crows are comfortable here
Whenever I look out
there they are
sitting on one window ledge or another

After it rained at night
two little frogs
hopped around the house
We couldn't figure out
how they got in

Finally we decided
they might have leapt from the clouds
and entered with the raindrops

16 JUNE 2015

123   The Crown

I was crowned today
A crown woven with breeze
and the timeless fragrance of wild flowers
The day is not far
When I will get back
the kingdom I lost

8 NOVEMBER 2015

124   On the Shores of Separation

Standing on the unbridgeable
shores of separation
I send my wife
a single kiss
as my gift
I am confident
she won't expect anything else
This is all I can offer her anyway

10 NOVEMBER 2015

125 Cups

I am turning fifty
The many-hued cups
from which I have drunk
lie in front of me

I know I am beyond help now
but still
a little bit of love for life
is left in these cups

Time asks me
that if I were offered the choice
to drink from just one of these cups
which one would I pick

No doubt
it would be that fourth cup
the one
I used to hold between my teeth
hoisted, sitting ball-crushed
on my mother's hip

10 NOVEMBER 2015

I was raised in an age
when the virtuous hero
ruled the roost everywhere
in films, in literature
in drama, in the neighbourhood
around the common well

When the smoke of vices blew my way
I gathered it, turned it into a genie
imprisoned it in a single jar
and placed it in a corner

Virtue is unharmed
But even as it spreads its fragrance around
a little fart emanates from within the jar
and penetrates the scent
I was always the first one to hold the nose
Since everyone cherished such a jar of their own
they quickly checked to see if the lid was shut

This is the age of vices
in films, in literature
in drama, in the neighbourhood
around the common well

After much effort
I trapped virtue inside the jar
and moved it elsewhere

I still have to hold my nose
when a fart emerges from within the jar
But I do so a little gladly

8 DECEMBER 2015

127 Everyone

I keep open all windows
and doors
and sit as darkness itself
listening to the rain
When I doze off
rocked by its rhythm
it tickles me awake
with a draught
Everyone
needs company

10 NOVEMBER 2015

128 Not Inside?

I have been in an island for ten days now
Floodwater is closing in on me on all sides
It can touch my feet any second now

Standing on the rooftop
I watch the floods at a safe distance
On a nearby television screen
I see submerged buildings breathing
through one nostril
Wails reach me in waves

I find some comfort in checking now and then
to see how close the flood's feet have reached
Ten days, three meals
tea three times a day
electricity, movie
neighbours to share these with
God has arranged
everything in advance
My job is only to take what's given

My anxiety doesn't stop me from taking what is on
    offer
Even the unfamiliar roar of the heavy rain
that scares me a little at first
soon turns into a lullaby

So that I don't disappoint the people
who call on my cell phone

'It's the flood all around,' I say in a worried voice
'It hasn't come into the house?' they ask
sounding expectant, almost disappointed

What can I do?
No, the flood
is not kind enough
to graze my feet

8 DECEMBER 2015

129   The Broken Leg

Early one morning
a one-legged crow sits/stands
on the clothes line on the terrace
resting after its search for food

Its broken leg dangles like a lizard's tail
Was it born this way?
Did it happen later?
Does it manage with one leg?
Can it fly properly?
How is it able to sit/stand
all night on one leg?

When it sees that I don't chase it away
even when it shits on me
it starts talking to me
Questions, queries, concerns
I respond, too

The crow comes every day now
With my words holding up its broken leg
it now sits/stands on two legs
that one-legged crow
No, no
simply the crow

9 DECEMBER 2015

130 Waking the Mind

Every day I wake up the puppy
that has curled up
in a corner it found
one rainy day

I call softly at first
Then keep calling until
my voice thunders
But I don't see even a small movement
I go near and push gently
with my hand
It buries its face into its body
and tenses up

Annoyed, I slap it hard
Then get up and kick
But all I get is a faint murmur

Should I try pouring water on it?
Should I drop a rock on its head
and kill it?

When waking
has come to murdering
what does it matter
whether it wakes up or not

13 DECEMBER 2015

131   Not Strong Enough

Thunder falls on my head
The earth trembles under my feet
Flowers wither at my touch
There is smoke under my nostrils
I am burning all over

My heart is not strong enough
to go on
living, staying
here

21 DECEMBER 2015

132 Unbearable

You keep aiming
little poison-tipped arrows
at me
It is unbearable
Why don't you kill me
with one big arrow?

21 DECEMBER 2015

133 Destiny

Destiny
Whose destiny?
Destined for whom?
Destined by whom?

There are no more questions
The flood has gone over my head

Destiny, please embrace me
for a moment
Let me bury my face in you

21 DECEMBER 2015

134   Which Finger?

With which finger did you write
my fate on my forehead?

The conceited thumb
The forefinger that points
The snake finger that hides
The ring finger for adornment
The puny little finger

Could you find no other head
to practise writing
with your blunt fingers?

21 DECEMBER 2015

135 O Time

On my back
bent by a life of burdens
you place a rock
and play rolling it round
and round
Do you have no pity
O Time?

21 DECEMBER 2015

136 Henceforth

Whatever I churn turns into poison
Henceforth, my tongue cannot tell the taste
even if a drop of nectar falls on it

21 DECEMBER 2015

137 The Rot

Standing around me
demons beat their breasts
I lie rotten
like a long-dead corpse

21 DECEMBER 2015

138 The Going

I am counting on the fact
that I know how to swim
I have enjoyed swimming in a well
A swim in the river, too, is pleasurable
I have leapt into a lake from its shores
I have wrestled with waves in the sea too

But
how can there be any swimming
in the roaring flood
that swells by the second?
Here
I have let myself go with the flood

21 DECEMBER 2015

139 The Dear Departed

There are many
who died in front of my eyes

Appucchi died
Grandfather, too, died
Father died
Grandmother died
Older brother died
Aunt died
Mother, too, died

They could at least have carried with them
this little kid on their shoulder or hip
Perhaps they didn't love me enough, after all

21 DECEMBER 2015

140 Dusk

Darkness arrives
like a mass
of rain-bearing clouds

It scrapes clean
the dense cavities of light
removes shades of difference
smears an ashen hue
and sits looking around

Then
it grows a wondrous paintbrush
and creates dark-coloured trees

Insects, birds
and other little creatures
turn into pieces of darkness
blend and dissolve

I leap out and leave
through the bars in the window
There is a rustle
in the dusk's painting of shadows

27 AUGUST 2015

141 My Day

I plan for a long time
to somehow make one day
entirely mine
When I wake up declaring
that the day is mine
I see that I am late, it has already started
When I get ready excitedly
and step out thinking this is my day
the legs of the cat that crosses my path
take the day with them

142 Darkness

I am a worshipper
of darkness

It pulled me up
when I fell
tripping on a stone

It dusted me off
nursed my wounds
washed my clothes
and even gave me
some solace

I grew strong
suckling at darkness's breasts
I asked of it
that inside and out
it shall be darkness everywhere

Darkness is my god

143 Thirst

A beast of unquenchable thirst
leaps out from within me

It savours for a moment the warmth
of blood splatter on its face
when it bites into a throat

The next moment
another throat
Blood splatter
Warmth
Then a leap towards another throat

It is never going to stop now
this insatiable beast

25 DECEMBER 2015

144 Finding God

I first found god
as a small piece of paper
I held him in my palm
showed him off to relatives
hid him inside a book

When I lost him somewhere
I shed tears
until I found him again

When I realized I couldn't protect him
any longer
I stuck him on the door
He now blesses everyone from there
He is free of worries
though a little faded

25 DECEMBER 2015

145 Every Day

Taking each step
on the ladder rungs
cautiously
very calmly
very, very patiently
I climb up slowly

The ground looks like an illusion
I can see plants that sit hiding
I can see electric poles
holding hands like a human chain
I can see the giant skeletons
of cell phone towers

Cautiously
calmly
patiently
I climb up slowly
Everything fades with dusk
Darkness spreads out in waves

Cautiously
calmly
patiently
I climb up slowly
I keep climbing up slowly

The day dawns
Light spreads brightly
I am lying on the ground

I recover
dust myself
rub my chest
motivate myself
and climb up slowly

Cautiously
calmly
patiently
I keep on climbing up
every day
on the rope ladder
that hangs from the sky

26 DECEMBER 2015

146 One's Own Place 1

This land where I belong is too hot
to even place my feet on it

The dust that stuck to me
the first time my feet touched it
The dust that I secretly ate with relish
until my stomach hurt
The dust that I have absorbed into my blood
rolling and playing
The dust that has digested
some of my relatives
The dust that is life

Seeds get roasted in this heat
A charred smell everywhere
Cracks appear all over my body
The smell of pus from boils
Heat envelops
and swallows from all sides

Like a bird flying away screaming
from a burning forest
I leave
There is no place any more
where I belong

30 DECEMBER 2015

147　One's Own Place 2

Many are the trodden trails
my feet have made here
Many are the paths
my ancestors have laid
and I have walked on
The dead-end lanes
and chariot streets are all
ways I know well
The highways that connect my world

I cannot walk these paths
any more

A giant frog
places its front feet out
for support and
leaps and lands outside
The ground between its feet
is what I can call mine

30 DECEMBER 2015

148 Hometown

Don't be in haste
to ask anyone
about their hometown

There might be people
who cannot tell you their hometown
There might be people
who dream about their hometown

There are, perhaps, people
who have forgotten their hometowns
There are, perhaps, people
who have left behind their hometowns

There could also be those
who stay, yet don't live
in their hometowns
There could even be those
who were chased away
by their hometowns

It is possible
that there are also those
who have no place
to call their own

30 DECEMBER 2015

149 Pack of Wolves

Words hounded me
like a pack
of ravenous wolves

I ran
legs folding under me
tongue gone dry
breath hot like fire
losing my bearings
I fell, rolled over
sprang up
and ran
all over the forest

Bleeding all over
from bite wounds
I fainted
and woke up later

A verdant sky opened its arms
Relief
I don't have to run any more
The wolves have gone elsewhere

28 JANUARY 2016

150   Inside the House

There is the house
with a lock on its door
with the key in a bag
the door latched on the inside

In the morning
the door opens
a little

It is locked shut
in the forenoon
when the heat is on the rise
It is opened
at night
only to be bolted up from the inside
right away

The thief
who entered the house
parting its thatched roof
one foggy moonlit winter night
was the first person to see

That there was nothing inside the house
But
he
didn't tell anyone

6 JANUARY 2016

151 Heat

My day lingers
in the afternoon
Perhaps it was born
slowly, very slowly
from darkness

Even though dawn arrived very late
and only after raining down at first
and wiping everything clean
it still brought new light

Then as the heat kept rising
it grew into a harsh summer day
The heat hasn't subsided
even in the afternoon
I am curious to see
how the rest of the day will be
It might cool down slowly
or just stay as it is

If the heat is meant to last
let the day end itself right here
Covered in laziness and languor
this day
looks like an ash-smeared body

7 JANUARY 2016

152   The Coward's Fear

The coward
is very scared

He is afraid even to open his eyes at dawn
even though
he didn't sleep all night
out of fear

He is scared of the bird that brings him news
He is scared of the rat that runs and hides in its hole
He is unable even to meet
the cat's gaze
Dogs chase him
Bulls come pointing their horns at him

He is afraid to walk
He is afraid to cross the road
Lamps explode
Walls close in on him

The earth trembles
The sky descends at great speed
and bangs against the earth
Stars swell and grow
and rain down as fire

He stays alive
hiding in a dark cave

hunched
eyes shut

But
what he is very
very, very
very scared of
are the human faces
that appear before him

7 JANUARY 2016

153   Looking Back

I had to climb up the hill
holding on to the crevices
between rocks
making a single trail of footprints
But now as soon as I reach the top
firebrands
rain down on me

Is this what I struggled for?

I had to crawl
stretched like a centipede
inching my way forward
through thorny woods
But now on the other side
a fearsome cave welcomes me
spreading out its matted locks

Is this the fruit of my journey?

I had to walk carefully
placing one step after another
as if in prayer
and leaping over mud
on the raised edges of fields
But now on the other side awaits
a wide open grave

Are all my efforts in vain?

I had to hide
becoming a speck
folding within a wave
swaying to its rhythm
and reach the ocean
But once there now
a large whale comes
swishing his tail about

I don't wish to live any longer

9 JANUARY 2016

154   A Lowly Worm

I am
a worm
a little worm
a lowly worm
a casual touch
a playful touch
the feeling of touch
whatever it is
fearing even
a slight touch
I curl
curl
curl and curl
I am a lowly worm
unable to cross
this small
burnt stretch
of land

10 JANUARY 2016

155   A Single Word

My dear
I am looking
in my feeble language
for one word to send you

In a single flick
it will fly to you
and clear away
your confusions

When uttered
it will become a spell
and drive away
your displeasure

It will hide in your handbag
and when it is opened spread
as the fragrance of flowers
and wash away
your wounds

It will become
a sparkling gem
and keep you company
in the dark

All I need
is that one word
a spell

13 JANUARY 2016

156   A Minor Discordance

My dear
the little discordant note
in your voice on the cell phone
becomes an arrow
and pierces deep
into my heart

It then pulls itself out
patiently
slowly
and aims next
for my brain

Once my brain is addled
it pierces
each cell in my body
at great speed

Blood-pouring body
Afflicted soul

13 JANUARY 2016

157   A Carpet of Flowers

My dear
it is true that your path
is a carpet of flowers
but
it is also strewn with thorns
as small as eyelashes

To look for them
I multiply thousandfold
these fingers of mine
that have played their part
in laying the path for you

But still
do walk carefully
Wear
thick leather shoes
Now walk
fearlessly

13 JANUARY 2016

158 My Language

It is older
than even sand and stone

It is a battery that has shored up
two thousand, three thousand, four thousand, five thousand
years of words
and keeps aglow its literary flame

A political, classical language
refined by alternating times
of light and dark

An immense language
of five hundred thousand words

But
in my language
silence squats firmly
in all those places
meant for my words

21 FEBRUARY 2016

159 Stone-Heavy

I cannot bear
the stone heaviness of this head
I bang it on the wall
Nothing happens
A mere cotton wall

I crash my head
on a rock
Nothing happens
Flower-soft rock

I dash my head
on the ground
Nothing happens
Fluid ground

What can I do
about this heavy protrusion of a head?
It goes giddy
and twirls
dashing repeatedly
against an airy expanse

23 FEBRUARY 2016

160 A Rush of Complaints

I sewed my lips tight shut
and let my ears bloom
and unfurl their petals

First a massive complaint
fell with a bang
Then several of them
lined themselves up
They She He
That This
My ears were stunned by this rush of complaints

Voices blended
There were complaints galore about me
I laughed listening to each of them

I spread out my earlobes like wings
Now
I am listening to the complaints
of the universe

25 FEBRUARY 2016

161 Calm

Write, they request
Write, they plead
Write, they insist
Write, they force
Write, they command
Write, they scream
Write, they beg

No one seems to notice
the rotten fingers I am showing them

The demand to write
grabs at my throat
with the same force
as the demand not to

Don't write, don't write
Write, write
Since neither of these
is meant for me
I stay calm

29 FEBRUARY 2016

162   Just a Little

I can't bear
the perpetual scowl on your face

The grin on your face
like a fruit fallen in shit
hurts my eyes

It is terrifying to see you
constantly ripping
and chewing at pieces of flesh
with bloodstained teeth

My ears are embittered
listening to your talk
that turns my language
into a stinking pile of words

Why is it that with each move
your hands
trip someone or another?
Why is it that at least in intent
your legs
are constantly kicking
someone or another?

You don't have to feed water
to the distressed birds that sit on the wall
But you shoo them away with a stick

You don't have to feed
the tired little lambs
some green from your thorny plants
But you could let them rest a while
under the tree that you didn't plant

You could relax your hold
a little
a little more
just a little bit more
just look at the fresh tip of the new shoot

3 MARCH 2016

163 This Is Your Problem

There is snot stuck inside your nose
In the shower, you use your little finger
to pick at it and fling it out
While washing your face
while wearing make-up
while combing your hair
you stand in front of the mirror
and poke and poke at it

But still
there is snot stuck inside your nose

In public, when no one is watching
you lower your head a little and pick your nose
Cleaning it with your handkerchief
breathing in hard, sneezing out—
you do all you can to remove it

But there is no end to this snot
You find some relief
only after you take some of it
and stick it on the noses you encounter

4 MARCH 2016

164 My Close Colleague

Last evening
I went to the beach
for some air
and to take in the scene

A murder took place
looking much like a game
of run and chase

A crowd dragged, by the hair
the people who sat in the shades of boats
taking turns to lie with their heads
on each other's laps
exchanging kisses
The crowd slapped them on their faces
punched them on their backs
and chased them away

Waves of people
kept appearing
to negotiate with those sitting alone

This wave that rose quietly at first
suddenly
grew sky-high
and ebbed only after
sweeping everything
into its underbelly

Terrified at the sight of the empty beach
I ran away

Earlier today
I described with panic
all of these
to my close colleague
Swallowing his diabetes pills
he asked me with a smile
'So you didn't get the fresh air you were seeking?'

4 MARCH 2016

165 A Fifty-Year Relationship

Once it came loose
after I bit and pulled at a corn on the cob
that little lower tooth
that had grown slanted
and jutting out a little
caused unbearable pain for a whole year

I went to get it extracted
only after my brain sat on the tooth
and pain became all-consuming
A single injection, a single pull
is all it took
A fifty-year relationship
A companion
And I didn't even get to see
the body

It left me
a little gap
that would no more be filled
with its presence

My first loss
was my milk tooth
the sight of which
had given my mother
so much joy

Whenever I look into the mirror
I grin wide
to see how big the gap is
And it opens itself wide and replies
that henceforth
it is time to lose
one
one
one by one

5 MARCH 2016

They come from the southern tip
they come from the midlands
they also come from the north
and they come from the west too

If you are up
for melting your body
and offering it in return
for three square meals a day
then you can pick any of these job balls
rolling in the streets
You can kick and play with them

If you are ready
to offer even your head
high iron gates
will open quickly
and suck you into
classrooms

You can work hard and prosper, come here
You can get an education and grow, come here
Plenty of work for very little pay
Come here
One day off in a month but no pay
Come here
You can collect chicken droppings, come here
You can carry rods, come here
You can clean tables, come here

If you have money, come here
You can sit in classrooms, come here

It has a place for servants
And for slaves too

24 MARCH 2016

167   A Cure for All Ills

Those who offered the crowd
talismans containing
their ideology, religion, alliances
started talking one after another
when they saw the gullible
looking keenly at what was on offer
The crowd kept nodding
in agreement

First
they made people understand
that their minds were layers of dregs
and showed them how to clean
They said their talismans alone
were the cure for all ailments
and looked for somewhere to tie them

They looked perplexed
at waists that had no string around them
waists that had not seen
a loincloth since childhood

Then
they just tied them to the tips of penises
and left looking pleased
Now
the crowd wanders swinging its talismans

24 MARCH 2016

The Right Way

for Rohith Vemula

Suicide
is the right way for us
To impress upon you
that we boycott
disregard
resist
your authority
your pride
your lust
your love
your concern
your sympathy
your power
your lowliness
your arrogance
your compassion
your pity
your alms
Suicide alone
is the right way for us

11 MARCH 2016

169 Magnanimity

for Rohith Vemula

His last words:
'I have no complaints against anyone
I blame no one
No one is responsible for my death'

It is we
who lack the dignity
to admit to everything

11 MARCH 2015

170 Ladies and Gentlemen

Escaping fire
we have come seeking refuge
in this city

We stand on our own feet
on ground that is no one's
When you step away
to answer nature's call
from the chairs on which
you sit spread-legged
we sit on their edges
and rest a little

Late in the desolate night
we catch naps
on lonely bus-stop benches

The leaves you cast aside are enough for us
The fruits you set aside are enough for us

When you are lost in your work
we catch a glimpse of the sun
we breathe in the air a little

We will never covet your crown
We can't even approach your throne

Therefore ladies and gentlemen

please don't deal out
the spray of poison through your sidelong glances
Please bear with us

19 MARCH 2016

171 Wagging Tongues

This is their full-time job

They can make
even the most righteous
spread open their thighs for them

Some keep their legs spread out all the time
For some, all it takes is a word to loosen up
Some look about them hesitantly
before opening their legs wide

Some are shy by nature
But these people are relentless
They are adept
at sending their magical tongues
that start from the feet
and slowly make their way up

Their tongues are like yercum leaves
warmed over a fire
to a perfect texture
Some like it rough
Some prefer soft
And if need be
they can use the sharp tip too

Those mouths are thirsty deserts
They don't discriminate between fresh and rotten

Mature ones work fast
but they need to be twisted to a stop
They are not satisfied easily
They kneel down and open their mouths
again and again
over and over

Youth springs up in rage
at their touch
It takes a long time
to calm it down and take it into the mouth
They are skilled at working up a froth
weakening it
making it go flaccid

What weapon can you possibly wield
against these thirsty tongues
that bend
fawn
soften
embrace
and mate
any time anywhere

19 MARCH 2016

172 A Bright Dawn

Since I wake up
to the chirping
of black birds
it always dawns bright for me
The glowing faces of trees
the flutter of bird wings
the sight of the first rays

In my spotless mind
a human face appears
with the first complaint
Then more and more faces
with more and more complaints

I listen to complaints
I respond to complaints
I ignore complaints
I handle complaints
I voice complaints
I gather complaints

Carrying my mind
like a sack of complaints
I enter the night
and sleep poorly
looking forward
to the brightness of dawn

17 MAY 2016

173   A Somewhat Old Country Hen

I am
a somewhat old country hen

I came of age, roamed around
looked for a fit rooster with whom I mated
and laid eggs every day without fail
I went mad brooding those eggs
making sure not one of them went to waste
I pushed them under me with my beak
I had plenty of chicks

Surrounded by my brood of chickens
bursting with pride
I stepped out to find food
Grains, termites, worms and insects
Scratching and digging the earth with my nails
I showed these to my little ones
It was their first feed
They pecked and ate with excitement

In that feeding frenzy, I failed to notice
the crow that caught a chick by its neck
and flew away like a shadow
I cried for help
and huddled my other chicks under me

We rested a while, and set out to find food again
When the crow descended this time
I lifted myself up as high as my wings would allow

and leapt and pecked at it
But many crows landed up from somewhere
and flew away with a chick in each beak
Not one was left

I now leap and fly as high as my wings allow
and suddenly fall to the ground
I have gone mad
A somewhat old country hen
that I am

17 MAY 2016

174 It Is Raining

It was only yesterday
that torrential rain
swept away the mounds of trash
and left everything clean

In a single night
enormous trash
has piled up again

This morning
it is raining again
But
a bit wearily

17 MAY 2016

175 Encountering Tears

It is perhaps the case
that at fifty
a man has to encounter tears every day

They are the same old complaints
but she finds it necessary now
to keep tears at the ready

When my son or daughter
want something from me
it unsettles me
to see tears of entreaty
welling up in their eyes

When I am out on the street
at least four or five tears
come rolling towards me and drown me
Among the many raised voices on the cell phone
at least one seems to end in tears every day

When I settle in front of the television
relieved at a day of no tears
some unremarkable scene
moves me to tears
tears I have to wipe away
without anyone noticing

17 MAY 2016

176 The Insatiable Begging Bowl

You seek alms
Carrying in your hand
an insatiable begging bowl
you seek alms

At first, unaware
I offered it rice as usual
Thinking it might reject leftovers
I filled it up with a fresh hot mound of rice

Hesitant
to offer it handed-down clothes
I filled it up with thousands of new ones
bought with blood, sweat and tears

What more could I offer
to this begging bowl
that has swallowed everything in a gulp

I tried offering it some lush red soil
I threw in some old gold treasures
Nothing sated its demonic appetite

I then picked up
my old shitty pride
that lay torn like an old slipper
in my trash
and flung it

like a dead rat
towards the bowl

The begging bowl bared a thousand teeth
grinned and caught it in its mouth
and was sated

18 MAY 2016

177   Happy Now?

It was just a whiff
but you caught the scent
and have landed up here

I have been hearing
your distressed sounds
since dawn
You terrify me with your barking
You warn me with your howls
You whimper and plead
You tug frantically at my thatched roof
with your blunt claws

Why are you after me
when there are many who are ready
to pamper you
and to stroke
your long, drooling tongue

You refuse to go away
When I aim a stone at you
to chase you away
you shrink and withdraw
and plead for protection
My arm aches
Wait, be patient for a little while

But you run in circles around me
led by your sharp sense of smell

Here, here
take these leftovers from my plate
Can you find
any bones and scraps?

Grab some with your teeth
and go stand at a distance
At least you get to eat in peace

Wretched dog!
Are you happy?
Happy now?

23 MAY 2016

178 The Secrets He Knew

Many are relieved
that the dead man
can no longer speak

The secrets he knew
are buried with him

Those who had believed
that he knew a secret
about them
and hence
had been hiding
are now gathered in celebration

It is a feast of secrets
that is going on

23 MAY 2016

179   About the Dead Man

They talk a lot

Some in their real sleep
Some in their fake sleep
Some mockingly
Some teasingly
Some in jealousy
Some in envy
Some in frustration
Some tearfully
Some obscenely
Some in censure
Some in praise
Some in slander

He is listening to everything
the dead one
the corpse

23 MAY 2016

180 The Dead Man Speaks

You might call this unnatural
but
the dead man speaks

The wind
lends its ears
Trees say hmm
Clouds agree
The moon laughs
Cuckoos respond
and urge him on
Owls are delighted

The dead man speaks
The dead man goes on speaking

But they have no fear at all
that he might voice grievances against them

25 MAY 2016

181 The Magical Finger

Now that the dead man speaks
and could reveal their secrets
they gather around and question him

Who are you?
One among you
Your family?
It is among yours
Your place
The same as yours

Cause of death
Silence
They ask over and over
Silence

They are unable to see
the magical finger
pointing at them

25 MAY 2016

182 Stay Put

Is this a new path or an old one I am walking
It is a little old and a little new
The new one is easier
I falter in the old one

There is no one ahead of me
So whether it leads to a garden or a desert
there will be the joy of discovery

Some people accompany me on the journey
Some others pretend to come along
There are those who struggle
unable to decide
one foot planted firmly somewhere
and the other dangling in mid-air

There are a few who follow me
There are a few who pretend to follow me
When I turn around
I see some feet that are truly rushing to catch up
There are also some feet that can't make up their minds

I did not invite anyone
I did not coerce anyone

It was you who waved and yelled
and begged to come along
At first, you kept pace with me
Then you said you'd come behind me

But when I turned back after a while
there you stood, a tiny dot, where you'd stood earlier

Stay there
Stay where
you are comfortable

Also feel free to complain
that the path is wrong
that I didn't take you with me

25 MAY 2016

183　Here I Am

Your desires are but few
but I am unable to fulfil any of them
When you express one hesitantly
I am gripped by fear
It appears as daunting as crossing
rivers of stones, thorns, water and fire

Your needs are little
but I still feign ignorance of them
When you let me know of one indirectly
I feel agitated
I feel a breathlessness
like I am caught forever
in the knots in a riddle

Here I am
utterly useless

2 JUNE 2016

184 I Don't Like These Dogs

for Sundara Ramasami

I don't like these dogs

They hide in little nooks
bark suddenly
and terrorize unsuspecting passers-by

Curled up next to a sewer pit
they wait for passers-by
Then they bare their teeth and growl
and chase them away

They pretend to pounce on some people
With some others, they make as if to bite
And all of them yearn to mate
with the one bitch
who runs covering her genitals with her tail

They run around barking within compound walls
When they can't get what they want, they howl and
    curse
They walk in circles as far as their chains would let
    them

They drool
for leftovers and bones
They curl their tails, twist their bodies
and show their loyalty

They eat and barf
and eat what they've barfed
They run covered in rashes
They breed like crazy

I don't like these dogs
They should have stayed in the wild
These wretched creatures

2 JUNE 2016

185 Pig, O Pig!

Don't be in a hurry
Don't follow me
Don't complain

If you get between my legs
and trip me over
how will you get what you want?
If you wait for me to squat
and crouch behind me right away
how will you get as much as you need?

You need me to feed you, don't you?
So be patient
wipe away your drool
exercise some self-control
close your eyes

Come now
Take and swallow
what I have left for you

Don't worry
I shall never deny you
what you need
what is yours
You will get some
tomorrow too
Just don't bother me
Be patient

3 JUNE 2016

186 Bare Hands

My dear
I desire
to make a bed of flowers
to spread a silk carpet
on your path

But all I have
are these hands
these bare hands
So I move in front of you
pushing aside stones
picking away thorns

6 JUNE 2016

187   Two Steps

My dear
I shall keep you company
for just two more steps
Within the first step
lies a swirling eddy where crocodiles gape
Within the next step
lies a pit that leads to hell
First walk with your gaze fixed on the sky
Then walk however you want

6 JUNE 2016

188 A Wide Open Space

In a wide open space, I was born
In a wide open space, I crawled
In a wide open space, I walked
In a wide open space, I ran
In a wide open space, I roamed
In a wide open space, I ate
In a wide open space, I shat
In a wide open space, I flew
In a wide open space, I copulated

When did
the wide open space
shrink
to a cage?
Whose hands control
the latch to the cage door?

19 APRIL 2016

189 The Thick-Skinned Buffalo

Tired of all these years of life
the thick-skinned buffalo
lies curled up
with its head between its legs

In the mild morning heat
sparrows sit on it
and peck at it
Such pleasure
the pleasure of scratching an itch

Then a large mosquito lands on it
moves all over its body
piercing over and over with its fine needle
Flies gather around
and enter its ears and nostrils
The buffalo unfurls its tail
and whirls it about slowly
Then laziness takes over again

A fox that happened to come by
throws a stone at the buffalo
No movement
So the fox runs to tell everyone
that the buffalo is dead
and brings a crowd

A leash of foxes surrounds it
But having seen through half-open eyes

the foxes baring their teeth
and getting closer
the buffalo lifts its tail
shakes its body
moves its horns
and stands up
in a leap

28 MAY 2016

190 Leg Pain

On that day when I had to run
in fear of strange threats
my dear son
travelled standing
for the five hours it took
to get from that town to this
in that rickety old train

He had never experienced
such a journey before
His young face hadn't seen
as much as a shadow of exertion
I made some room between my legs
and asked him to sit

He was shy
I was grieving

Even though I travelled squatting
in a little gap
my leg still hurts

10 JUNE 2016

191 Curse

Your legs should break
May your right leg be smashed to smithereens
May your left leg dangle irreparably
May you realize what it means to be crippled

Your hands should just drop away from your body
May your fingers swell and explode
May worms crawl deep inside them
May you realize what writing is

You should go blind
May you struggle to find helping hands
May you touch everything and weep
May you know what it means to have sight

Your tongue should be chopped off
May you howl in vain
May your tongue lie numb like a corpse
May you come to know what a word is

Neither telling
nor showing
will make you understand

11 JUNE 2016

192 My Voice

At the touch of a mysterious finger
my throat closed in
and I lost my voice

Immediately you spoke
in my voice from somewhere
You spoke for me
You raised your voice
My voice in capitals
My voice in cities
My voice on highways
My voice on big streets
My voice in halls and conferences
My voice in magazines
My voice on television debates
My voice from far, far away

In my small city
in my little town
in my cross street
in my front porch
my voice
was simply absent

11 JUNE 2016

193   Why Do You Do These Things?

Why do you do these things?

You abuse someone for their caste
You provoke someone to abuse another for their caste
You get close to someone for their caste
You push someone away for their caste

Why do you do these things?

You make someone evil for his caste
You make someone good for his caste
You protect someone for their caste
You kill someone for their caste

Why do you do these things?

You gather crowds in the name of caste
You disperse crowds in the name of caste
You like someone for their caste
You hate someone for their caste

Why do you do these things?

You write a book in the name of caste
You burn a book in the name of caste
You make up stories in the name of caste
You challenge stories in the name of caste

Why do you do these things?

You make money in the name of caste
You lose money in the name of caste
You attain power in the name of caste
You snatch power in the name of caste

Why do you do these things?

You find identity through your caste
You destroy identity in the name of caste
You wield authority in the name of caste
You submit to authority in the name of caste

Why do you do these things?

When will you realize
that your minds are shackled?

11 JUNE 2016

194 There Is Enough

This is what occurs to me
often these days:
what I have is enough

The great works of literature
grammars
theories
dissertations
stacked in my own library
Aren't these enough?

A lifetime is hardly enough
to read and learn everything

And three-fourths of that time
is shared with ants
that drag these away
in little pieces

Enough
What I have is enough

But still
when a single word
from the present
comes and bites me
I do jump up in shock

11 JUNE 2016

195 No One

That was the day
loneliness
pulled me into a tight embrace

Laziness
lay wide awake

Meal
was just two fruits
The time of the day
moved relishing the quiet
There was no one else
No one stopped by
No one spoke

There is pleasure
only in being alone

14 JUNE 2016

196 This Is Enough

Like a giant hand coming to rest
the vehicle came to a stop

They prostrated
They genuflected
They got up and made way
They stooped and cowed
They shrank and shrivelled

This is all they ever want
This is forever enough
for them

14 JUNE 2016

197 You and I

You live
in a stinking pit
Unaware of the tug
of the magical chain
you lie curled up inside
You drool when you are hungry
Crusty-eyed, you lick off
leftover and spoiled food
from the plate within your reach
Then you curl up again

Sometimes you get some bones
On those days, to show your gratitude
you wiggle your body
An occasional bark
to point out a visitor
A whimper of gratitude

I have nothing
to say to you

16 JUNE 2016

198   The Call

Knowing it will be hard to drag the sheep by the rope
the shepherd runs ahead of it
calling out in the voice he uses at feeding time
Thinking it is going to be fed
the sheep holds on to his voice and leaps and runs
towards the mirage

17 JUNE 2016

199 They Are Just Thirsty

Shepherds stand around
to keep the sheep from running away
But they needn't worry
The sheep are just thirsty

18 JUNE 2016

200 The Shepherd

With rope-shackles between their necks and feet
the sheep graze on the bund, bent in fear
The shepherd is in the shade
And beyond the bund, a lush green field

The shepherd raises his voice
to threaten the sheep that considers trespassing
The shepherd flings a stone
at the sheep that tries to cross over
The shepherd whips out his stick
towards the sheep that crosses over

The shepherd ties up the sheep
that continues to disobey
The shepherd shuts up in an enclosure
the sheep that pulls and breaks its rope-shackles
The shepherd appoints a dog
to watch over the sheep
that bleats around the enclosure
The shepherd sends to the butcher
the sheep that climbs over the fence
Sheep never change
Nor do shepherds

17 JUNE 2016

201 The Little Lamb

The shepherd
shuts the lamb
in an upturned basket
and takes its mother to graze
The little lamb can see nothing
but its own hunger

18 JUNE 2016

202 Competition

Announcement
Advertisement, Application
Millions and millions of applicants
Exam
Interview
Find the right person
Bribe, Bargain

There is insane competition
for a goatherd's job

18 JUNE 2016

203 Pity Is Still Alive

Fresh food to eat
Its own hole under the bush
Days and nights of busy wandering
Its own familiar pathways

The rat lost all that it had
and got caught in a trap

Pity is still alive

Hands that couldn't bring themselves
to kill the rat with a hook or
to drown it in water
carried the trap out
and opened it in a barren expanse

It took a little while
for the rat to sense its freedom
and run out
A vast expanse
an empty field
a hard ground
and a harsh sun

The rat now runs
looking anxiously at the spots
where the shadows of crow wings fall

19 JUNE 2016

204 Never

The moment of sorrow creeps in
even before
the moment of happiness is over

I never get to feel
anything fully

19 JUNE 2016

205 The Battlefield

I have

no sword to wield
no spear
no arrow to aim

no elephants to unleash
no horses
no soldiers to command

no kingdom
no enemies

Nevertheless
I set out from home
to the battlefield
every day
armed
armoured
with a battle plan
and an army

20 JUNE 2016

206 First, and Then

First
you try to smother me
with a shower of flowers
Then
you try to suffocate me
with a basketful of shit

But I dwell
in a vast, untouched space

22 JUNE 2016

207 A Flower

A flower blooms
after the big bang

A sharp scent
a fresh appearance
an electric radiance

A flower
that will reveal
and establish everything

22 JUNE 2016

208 The Dog I Used to Know

The dog I used to know has now gone rabid

The dog that used to show gratitude by wagging its tail
The dog that used to show its affection
by twisting its body and nuzzling against my legs
The dog that showed its loyalty
by licking my hand with its reddish tongue

The dog I used to know has now gone rabid

That dog that used to guard the house
The dog that would come to the street
to see me off
The dog that would wait for me on my return
and run and climb on me

The dog I used to know has now gone rabid

The dog that used to wait
for leftovers at mealtimes
The dog that would even risk its life
for a bit of leftover food
The dog that would clean up
even its own vomit

The dog I used to know has now gone rabid

The dog that knew when to stay away
The dog that knew who the enemies were

and to bare its teeth and chase them away
The dog that could sense my wish
and run and grab my kill in its teeth

The dog I used to know has now gone rabid

I now run away from its gaze
I am hiding
weapon ready at hand
waiting for the right time to kill it

26 JUNE 2016

209 What Have I Lost?

I spend entire days
staring at the corner of the roof
I lie pressed down
by the emptiness of space around me

Why?
What have I lost?

Was I used to wearing
an emperor's crown?
Had I stood with my feet
on the heads of thousands of slaves?

Do I like wearing a crown?
Am I happy ruling over slaves?

Then
what have I lost?

Did I lie caught in enchanting words
like a bee fallen in honey?
Was I trapped and submerged
in soft prayerful voices?

Is it praise that I need?
Is it worship that I want?

Then
what is it that I have lost?

Am I not one
who has lost everything
but still hasn't lost himself?

4 JULY 2016

210 Judgement Day

I anxiously await
the word
that will soon issue forth
from the lips of God

God's language
only has
good words, doesn't it?

5 JULY 2016

Growing Out of the Cocoon*

Greetings.

I'd never have imagined that my book—and especially one written in my mother tongue—would be launched in the capital city of India. I have mixed feelings on this occasion. I cannot but be unhappy about the circumstances that occasioned this. However, I cannot turn my back in sadness.

During the nightmarish time when my life was driven into a crisis following the controversy over my novel, *Madhorubhagan*, writers—from Tamil Nadu, from other parts of India and from across the world—stood by me, extending their support in various ways. Across the country voices were raised in support of freedom of expression and against intolerance. It is those voices which have brought me here today. I accepted this invitation to speak here only to express my gratitude to those voices.

I've always been averse to spectacle and sensation. A peasant cultural tradition that lives cloistered within its village is what shaped my disposition. I led a contented life in an out-of-the-way small town and was pursuing interests close to my heart. But circumstances have thrust me today to the capital city. This cannot but be without cause for regret.

It's difficult to say when I started writing. I was probably eight or nine then. A little ditty about my favourite cat, '*Poonai nalla poonai*', is the first writing that I can recollect. Some years later it was broadcast in the children's programme of All India Radio's Tiruchirappalli station. Since then poetry has been my primary vehicle of expression. It's later that my interests diversified into the short story, the novel and other prose forms. Barely a year separated

---

* Perumal Murugan's statement in New Delhi on 22 August 2016 on the occasion of the launch of his new book of poems, *Kozhaiyin Paadalgal*. Translated from the Tamil by A.R. Venkatachalapathy.

the writing of my first two novels. My third novel took seven years. Short and long intervals have punctuated my prose writings. During such intervals there've been times when I never wrote a line of prose. But there has not been a time when I didn't write poetry. I'd keep scrawling something or the other. Later I would reject some of these lines as mere scribbling; sometimes I'd wonder at their beauty.

Four volumes of my poems have been published so far, and they probably contain some hundred and fifty poems. These were the ones that passed muster. But in this, my fifth collection, there are over two hundred poems. Looks like some kind of alchemy was at work within me. I write poems for myself. Writing poetry is a private act. This is why only a small part of my poems have seen print.

Even in the midst of writing prose some poetic line would lead me away. Between December 2014 and June 2016 I couldn't so much as scratch a line in the first three months. As though the fingers of my heart had become numb. I couldn't read a thing. Even when I opened the newspaper my eyes would scan the print but my mind would not absorb a word. I'd flip through the pages like an illiterate person and fold it away. I consoled myself that there were things to do in this world other than reading and writing. And I did my best to turn my attention to them. But it was impossible. It was then that I realized the full meaning of the Tamil phrase 'nadaipinam', 'a walking corpse'.

Towards the end of February 2015 I went to Madurai to see my daughter, and spent a few days in my friend's house. On the first floor were two rooms. One was stacked with books and the other had a bed. With nothing to do I lay dazed night and day. I wallowed in a dark hole without the urge to see or talk to anybody. But as I ruminated over my existence, there came a certain instant when the sluice gates were breached. I began to write. I chronicled the moment when I felt like a rat, dazzled by the light, burrowing itself into its hole. I've always felt like a rat living in its hole. At that instant this image felt rather apt. There are a thousand alleyways in the burrow. And a thousand pockets too. The poems ended thus.

> Thousands of alleyways.
> Thousands of pockets.
> Amongst the pockets
> that no one can spot
> where am I
> now?

This beginning branched into innumerable ways. I wrote whenever anything struck me. As I started to write, I began to revive little by little, from my fingernails to my hair. It was poetry that saved me. *Kozhaiyin Paadalgal*, 'a coward's poems', is a book of such poems.

I have resumed my writing with poems. I've begun to relive my days, starting from my boyhood. Poetry continues to be the form of my liking. I'm not sure if these are good times for poetry. But it's poetry that has inaugurated my good times. Just as before, my writing could start from poetry and move into other forms. I believe that this is how it will happen. I am, however, unable to say *when* this will occur. It may happen step by step. Perhaps not at all. So what? Poetry will do for me.

I'd declared earlier that I believe in neither resurrection nor in reincarnation. I'm now confused: Should I start having such a belief? The Madras High Court has said that 'Time is a great healer' and that 'Time also teaches us to forget and forgive. If we give time its space to work itself out, it would take us out to beautiful avenues.' The learned judges have also said, 'Perumal Murugan should be able to write and advance the canvas of his writings.' The last word of the verdict—'write'—sounds to me both as a command and as a benediction.

The question of whether a word or a sentence in a judicial verdict should determine if I write or not remains in my mind. If a faceless force can put a full stop to writing, can't a line in a judicial verdict bolster writing? Moreover, the imperative 'write' suits my present state of mind and is cause for happiness. I've therefore resolved that I should thank the court, resume writing and start publishing. The publication of this book marks this beginning.

I am also mulling over the reissue of my earlier writings. I will soon begin the weary task of reviewing my books. If required I shall revise the text. I'm not sure if this is right. However, when so many things that are not quite right are happening all over, why not this? What am I to do? A censor is seated inside me now. He is testing every word that is born within me. His constant caution that a word may be misunderstood so, or it may be interpreted thus, is a real bother. But I'm unable to shake him off. If this is wrong let the Indian intellectual world forgive me. The learned judges have said that I should not live under fear. But my old teacher, the great Thiruvalluvar has said,

> Folly meets fearful ills with fearless heart;
> To fear where cause of fear exists is wisdom's part.
>
> (Translation by G.U. Pope)

Let me add something. Call it a request if you will. My mind has now attained a state of being able to write poetry. I need to maintain this state, and progress towards writing in other genres. Some years ago, on a happy evening, my two children asked me, 'Appa, how many books will you be writing?' 'How can I say that with any certainty?' I replied. But they pestered me. 'Okay then, tell us the books you have in your mind!' Until then I'd never contemplated such an exercise. I began listing out the books conceived in my heart. It came to about a fifty. Of these, over ten were novels. I was overcome with excitement. Would I live that long, I wondered? I reassured myself that 'My writing will do little to change this world. Let me write what I can.'

I'm not now sure that I will write every one of those fifty-odd books. Even if I do I doubt if they will take the same shape as conceived earlier. It's, however, certain that my writing will not be the same. To spell out what would be the nature of that change will require quiet and reflection. I need time to gather my creative energies. I'm not a motor pump to draw water from the depths the moment it is switched on. I'm more a pupa in a cocoon. It will require time to develop colourful wings. Please allow me the time to do so.

Taking the podium or giving interviews has never enthused me. I've given the occasional short interview. It is silence that gives me strength now. I'll write to gain further strength. My request therefore to the media and organizers of lit fests is this: 'Please do not ask me to speak. Let me be quiet. And write. I shall speak to you through my written words.'

My heartfelt thanks to all those who arranged this event and the audience who took part.